How to Save Money on Healthcare

Laura Town and Karen Hoffman

Omega Press
Zionsville, IN 46077

ISBN: 978-1-943414-08-6

Production Credits:
Authors: Laura Town and Karen Hoffman
Contributors: Sean Dixon and Rachael Mann
Publisher: Omega Press
Photos: All credited images used under license from Shutterstock.com

Social media connections:
Laura Town
Twitter: @laurawtown
LinkedIn: https://www.linkedin.com/in/lauratown

Omega Press in the News

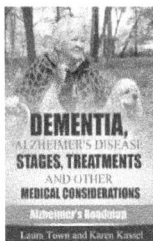

Dementia, Alzheimer's Disease Stages, Treatments, and Other Medical Considerations

- One of Book Authority's best books on dementia of all time
- One of Book Authority's best audiobooks on dementia of all time
- Audiobook recognized as a resource by the Alzheimer's Association
- Recommended by Dementia Insight
- Recommended by Alzheimer's Proof website
- Audiobook, ebook, and paperback available where books are sold

....

Long-Term Care Insurance, Power of Attorney, Wealth Management, and Other First Steps

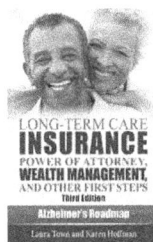

- One of Book Authority's best new insurance books to read in 2020
- Audiobook, ebook, and paperback available on Amazon

....

Nutrition for Brain Health: Fighting Dementia

- A Seniorlink 50 Essential Read for Anyone Coping with Alzheimer's Disease (www.seniorlink.com
- Audiobook, ebook, and paperback available on Amazon

CONTENTS

Chapter 1:
Costs of Care

It's no secret that healthcare in the United States is expensive. People of all ages and from all socioeconomic backgrounds face the reality that an unexpected illness or injury could be financially devastating. The problem is widespread, and it affects people with and without insurance alike. In fact, an estimated 57 percent of insured Americans have received unexpected medical bills for services not covered by their insurance. The costs of the care itself, the complexity of the billing process, and the confusing and overwhelming nature of the healthcare system all contribute to the fact that healthcare costs are crippling the country.

A trip to the emergency room costs an average of $1,917, but it can easily be thousands of dollars higher depending on the reason for the visit and the type of services provided. The cost of basic supplies can vary widely from one facility to another,

Credit: Evlakhov Valeriy

with some hospitals having markups over 1000 percent on these items. For patients, this translates into unbelievably high itemized costs, like $15 per pill Tylenol, $53 per pair non-sterile gloves, and $23 each alcohol swabs. Most hospitals are not openly transparent about their charges, leaving their patients angry and confused about how they are going to pay for what is often straightforward care.

The popular press is full of examples of patients who've received medical bills above and beyond what was expected for the treatment they received: the man in Connecticut who was billed $629 to bandage his child's finger, the woman in New Jersey who received a $5,751 bill for an ice pack given to her in the waiting area of the emergency room, the California woman who was charged $20,243 for care related to a bicycle accident that broke her arm. In the latter case, the woman was taken by ambulance to the nearest emergency room, which happened to be out of her insurance network. The woman's insurer paid what it deemed fair and reasonable for the services provided, leaving her responsible for more than $20,000 for a cast, a CT scan, and some pain medication. Unfortunately, her situation is not unique—in emergencies, patients often wind up at out-of-network facilities because they are the fastest and easiest to reach. Emergency rooms and out-of-network facilities are not the only culprits, however. In areas with few care providers to choose from, bills are often high due to the fact that the existing providers have a near-monopoly on healthcare.

The good news is that lawmakers are working on legislation that will decrease the likelihood of unexpected, high medical bills. Bipartisan groups in Congress are looking specifically to curb the costs associated with emergency care rendered by out-of-network providers when the patient is unable to pick their provider. They are also interested in changing requirements related to elective surgery by out-of-network providers at in-network facilities. Whether or not these changes come to pass, however, remains to be seen.

So, what can you—as a financially conscious healthcare consumer—do? First, you can work to understand the resources you have available to help pay for care. Second, you can look for ways to minimize the cost of your care. Finally, you can learn to decode your medical bills and be an advocate for yourself when errors have been made. This book will help you take these steps.

Terminal and Long-Term Care

While all healthcare is expensive, the cost associated with a terminal illness—and long-term care in general—is extremely high. According to the National Center for Chronic Disease Prevention and Health Promotion, 90 percent of the nation's $3.3 trillion annual healthcare costs involves two populations of patients: patients with mental health conditions and patients with chronic (long-term) health conditions. The cost of cancer care alone is expected to reach nearly $174 billion in 2020; obesity costs $147 billion annually; arthritis and related conditions cost in total $304 billion in 2013. The costs of persistent illness, terminal or otherwise, are staggering. These costs involve a number of things: treatment, diagnostic procedures, visits to the doctor, hospital stays, treatment of associated conditions that arise in the course of the illness, and on and on. Typically, care costs are lower in the early and mild stages of any illness and progressively increase as your needs become greater. Therefore, you need to know what to expect and what resources are available to you to help pay for adequate care.

Care costs for a person with a terminal illness are split into two categories: medical expenses and non-medical expenses. Different resources are available to help pay for each category of care. Medical expenses are usually partially paid by insurance, such as private health insurance, long-term care insurance, Medicare, or Medicaid, as well as by personal funds. Non-medical expenses are usually paid using personal funds. Also, remember that the cost of caring for multiple conditions at one time adds to the cost of care. Care costs vary by region and by medical needs. However, many individuals with a terminal illness face the same types of expenses, which are detailed in the following checklists.

Checklist: Medical expenses

- ☐ Doctors' visits (including specialists)
- ☐ Laboratory/diagnostic tests
- ☐ Hospital stays
- ☐ Medical procedures
- ☐ Medical equipment (e.g., walker or cane)
- ☐ Therapy (physical, occupational, speech)
- ☐ Prescription medications
- ☐ Personal care supplies (e.g., for incontinence)
- ☐ Insurance premiums

Checklist: Living expenses

- ☐ Adult day care (median, $70 per day)
- ☐ Home health aide (median, $22 per hour)
- ☐ Basic services in assisted living facility (median, $3,750 per month or $45,000 per year)
- ☐ Semi-private room in nursing home (average, $235 per day or $85,775 per year)
- ☐ Private room in nursing home (average, $267 per day or $97,445 per year)

Checklist: Non-medical expenses

- ☐ Basic costs of living

- ☐ Increased costs for activities you used to do on your own (e.g., home or vehicle maintenance, lawn care, driving, cooking)

- ☐ Home services (e.g., homemaker services, companion services, personal care services)

- ☐ Home safety modifications

- ☐ Emergency alert system

- ☐ Financial protection tools (e.g., different phone or P.O. Box to help avoid scams, identity theft protection)

- ☐ Taxes and fees associated with transferring wealth

- ☐ Attorney fees for creating legal documents or mediating court proceedings

- ☐ Counseling costs for the individual with a terminal illness as well as caregivers, family, and friends

Whether you have long-term or standard care needs, knowing what options are available to help pay for care can seem overwhelming when the bills start pouring in. The following sections detail many resources and options that can help lessen the financial burden of paying for care

Chapter 2:
Types of Insurance

The best way to help manage healthcare costs—particularly those associated with terminal illness—is to have quality health insurance and long-term care insurance policies. It is important to identify and purchase these policies while you are in good health. If you wait until you have been diagnosed with a long-term illness, a new health insurance policy may not cover it because it is a pre-existing condition. It is also likely that you will be ineligible for long-term care insurance if a policy is not already in place when the diagnosis is made.

Credit: Valeri Potapova

Without good health and long-term care insurance policies, you will have to spend down almost all of your assets before you are eligible for Medicaid. To prevent this from happening, the checklists in this book will guide you through financial options for paying for care, from private assets and insurance policies to public programs like Social Security, Medicaid, and Medicare.

Insurance Benefits

Healthcare costs are a substantial expenditure for many families. Whether for planned preventive care or unexpected illnesses or accidents, the amount of money spent each year quickly adds up. For an individual with chronic terminal illness, care costs can seem insurmountable, especially without adequate insurance.

Many individuals have a private health insurance policy to help pay for healthcare costs. For some individuals, this policy is available through their employer. Others have an individual policy. For people who have quit a job that offered insurance—whether due to a diagnosis or for another reason—COBRA insurance may be an option. Retirees often have health insurance through Medicare and/or Medicare supplemental plans. Low-income individuals may qualify for Medicaid.

Other than Medicaid, none of these insurance options provide benefits for long-term care for chronic terminal illness. If you don't want to spend down your assets to be eligible for Medicaid and you are concerned about the need for long-term care in the future, you may want to consider a long-term care insurance policy.

Private Health Insurance

Of the methods that Americans use to pay for healthcare, private health insurance is one of the most significant resources for families. Most health insurance policies cover medical costs associated with accidents, sudden illness, and terminal illness, as well as doctors' visits, exams, lab tests, and medications. However, private health insurance generally does not cover home healthcare or long-term care. The following checklists address some of the things you should consider regarding private health insurance.

Checklist: Basics about private health insurance

☐ If you already have health insurance, you may have individual or family private insurance, a group employee plan or pension, or retiree coverage. Group plans always have less expensive premiums and often have better benefits than individual policies, although group plans are typically provided by employers and may not be available if you've quit or retired from your job.

☐ If you do not have health insurance, most private health insurance companies offer plans to individuals, although they may be prohibitively expensive. If you have a low income, purchasing a plan through the Affordable Care Act Marketplace may offer cheaper premiums.

☐ Previously, many new health insurance policies would not cover pre-existing conditions, although this has changed since the Affordable Care Act was passed. Before changing insurance plans or purchasing a new health insurance policy, make sure the new policy will cover your healthcare needs without discrimination.

☐ Private health insurance policies differ in monthly premium based on the deductible, co-payments or co-insurance, and type of coverage.

☐ The premium is the monthly amount the policy holder pays to the insurance company in exchange for insurance coverage.

☐ Premiums often depend on the types of services or conditions covered. For example, coverage for pregnancy and childbirth typically increases the premium. If you have pregnancy and childbirth coverage and are too old to have children, you may ask the insurance company to remove that coverage in exchange for a lower premium.

☐ A deductible is the amount of money the policy holder must pay out-of-pocket for medical expenses before the insurance company will begin to pay. For example, with a $6,000 deductible, you would have to pay the first $6,000 of covered services.

☐ A co-payment (or co-pay) is the amount charged directly to the policy holder for specific medical expenses (e.g., a $20 co-pay for every doctor's appointment).

☐ Co-insurance is similar to co-pays, except it is generally a percentage of the total cost (e.g., pay 10% of the cost of prescription medication).

☐ Co-payments and co-insurance are usually charged and paid up front at the time the expense is incurred.

☐ Many health insurance policies include some type of prescription coverage, although the out-of-pocket amount paid for generic drugs versus brand name drugs varies widely among policies, drugs, insurance companies, and pharmacies.

☐ Some private health insurance policies allow the use of a health savings account, through which medical costs can be paid for tax free. However, to qualify for an HSA, you must have a health insurance plan (as of 2020) with a deductible of at least $1,400 for an individual or $2,800 for a family; you can't have any other health insurance coverage, not even Medicare; and no one else may claim you as a dependent for tax purposes. Individuals can contribute up to $3,500 per year to an HSA and families can contribute up to $7,100.

☐ Other than the co-pay or co-insurance, most medical facilities and pharmacies will submit your medical claims to the insurance company on your behalf. The amount that is not covered by the insurance company is then billed to you. Full costs of medical services do not need to be paid at the time of service.

☐ Before the Affordable Care Act, most health insurance policies had an annual and/or lifetime maximum. Any medical costs over that maximum were the responsibility of the policy holder. However, now these maximums are not allowed for most new policies. If you have had the same insurance policy for many years, you may want to check if it has any maximum payouts associated with it. If it does have an annual or lifetime maximum, you may want to negotiate with the insurance company to have those limits removed.

If you have trouble paying for medical expenses even with a good health insurance policy in place, talk to medical facilities and providers and work out an affordable payment plan to pay for medical

Credit: Monkey Business Images

expenses. Most hospitals and clinics are willing to work with you if it means they will eventually get paid.

If you received health insurance through your job and have left that job, you may be able to extend your health insurance coverage through COBRA (Consolidated Omnibus Budget Reconciliation Act) for a limited time. For-profit companies with 20 or more employees and state and local governments that offer a group plan to employees are required to offer COBRA insurance when an employee's insurance coverage would typically end.

Checklist: Basics about COBRA health insurance

☐ COBRA insurance is very expensive. You will likely have to pay more than you were as an active employee because you will be paying both the employer and employee portions of the premium. In addition, the insurance company may charge an extra 2% for administrative fees and an extra 50% if you have a qualifying disability.

☐ COBRA coverage typically extends to all individuals who were previously covered on the insurance plan, including the former employee and the employee's spouse and dependents.

☐ Individuals who are eligible for COBRA insurance have 60 days from the time the employer plan ends to enroll in COBRA.

☐ COBRA coverage typically lasts 18 months, can be extended to 29 months in the event of disability, and can extend to an absolute maximum of 36 months.

☐ If you are eligible for COBRA insurance, you should consider all other health insurance options before you opt for COBRA coverage simply because of the increased cost of premiums. In particular, if your spouse and/or dependents are listed on the original policy, they should purchase a different policy as soon as possible, especially if they do not have pre-existing conditions.

☐ COBRA insurance is often useful if you plan to purchase a different policy but coverage on the new policy doesn't begin until one or more months after enrollment. In this situation, COBRA coverage would allow the individual or family to have uninterrupted health insurance coverage between plans.

☐ If you decide to waive your right to enroll in COBRA coverage, you are allowed to revoke your waiver any time within the election period (typically 18 months). Continued coverage then begins on the day the waiver is revoked and extends until the end of the original election period.

☐ If you terminate COBRA coverage before you have another insurance plan in place, you may not be eligible to receive insurance until the next open enrollment session, which is typically between November and January for most group plans.

☐ If your family does not want to use COBRA coverage, individuals on the terminated insurance plan have a 30- to 60-day special enrollment eligibility for other plans, starting from the day the insurance policy was terminated (for example, if a husband was listed on his wife's group plan and the wife was diagnosed with a terminal illness, they would have 30 days to enroll in the husband's group plan, if available).

Medicare

For retired people and some individuals with chronic terminal illness, many medical expenses are covered by insurance provided through Medicare. Medicare is a multi-part government insurance program for individuals who are 65 years of age or older, are under the age of 65 with

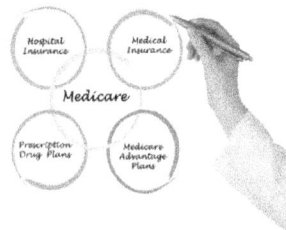

Credit: arka38

13

certain disabilities (including long-term illness if you are no longer able to work), or have end-stage renal disease.

The costs associated with Medicare coverage depend on several factors, including when you enrolled, the type of plan (or plans) chosen, work history, amount of income, medications needed, and providers used. The following checklists provide basic information about Medicare, including information about costs to expect. All costs are based on 2020 estimates unless otherwise noted. Estimates change each year, so check the Medicare website for the most up-to-date information.

Checklist: Types of Medicare coverage

☐ **Medicare Part A (Hospital Insurance).** Part A covers inpatient hospital stays, care in skilled facilities, hospice, and some home healthcare.

☐ **Medicare Part B (Medical Insurance).** Part B covers certain doctors' services, outpatient care, medical supplies, and preventive services. (Note: The term "Original Medicare" refers to Part A and/or Part B. These two parts are typically purchased together.)

☐ **Medicare Part C (Medicare Advantage Plans).** An Advantage Plan is a type of Medicare plan offered by a private company that contracts with Medicare to provide all of an individual's Part A and Part B benefits. Part C plans may also provide Part D benefits.

☐ **Medicare Part D (Prescription Drug Coverage).** Part D adds prescription drug coverage to Medicare Part A and Part B. Part D plans are offered by private insurance companies approved by Medicare.

Checklist: Basics about Medicare Part A and Part B

☐ You can find out whether you are eligible for Medicare by age by using the government's online calculator. You can also get an estimate of the premium amount and find out when the next enrollment period is if you are not already enrolled.

☐ When you enroll in Medicare, you are automatically signed up for Medicare Part A.

☐ Medicare Part B coverage is optional based on the presence of additional coverage. For example, if you are still working and are receiving health insurance through an employer or a spouse's employer, you can elect to not enroll in Medicare Part B. If you were automatically enrolled in Part B and you want to drop your coverage, you need to follow the instructions on your Medicare card. However, you may have to pay a late enrollment fee if you want to sign up again later.

☐ If you are receiving Social Security checks, you are automatically enrolled in Medicare Part A and Part B. People who qualify for Social Security disability are automatically enrolled two years after their disability is recognized. Individuals who are automatically enrolled will be sent a Medicare card upon enrollment.

☐ If you are not automatically enrolled, you will need to sign up in your Initial Enrollment Period. The seven-month Initial Enrollment Period is open three months before an individual's 65th birthday month, during the birthday month itself, and three months after. For example, an individual with a birthday in August will be eligible for enrollment from May 1 to November 30 in the year of their 65th birthday.

☐ If you miss your Initial Enrollment Period, you can sign up during the General Enrollment Period between January 1 and March 31 each year. You may have to pay a fee for late enrollment.

☐ Exceptions to the Initial Enrollment Period and General Enrollment Period occur if you did not enroll in Part B because you were in an employer or union group health plan. In that case, you can sign up for Medicare up to eight months after your coverage with the group health plan ends or after employment ends, whichever happens first. This usually does not incur a late enrollment penalty.

☐ You can apply for Medicare by visiting the Social Security website, going to the local Social Security office, or calling Social Security at 1-800-772-1213.

☐ You cannot be denied Medicare coverage because of your diagnosis with a terminal illness. If you are denied coverage and you believe you qualify because of age or disability, you are entitled to an individual analysis of eligibility. You may have better success obtaining coverage after denial if you ask your doctor to help.

☐ Fill out an Initial Enrollment Questionnaire (IEQ) so that your healthcare bills are paid correctly and on time. The form asks about other health insurance that might pay before Medicare does, such as group health plan coverage from an employer. Medicare will mail instructions for how to access and fill out this form online. You will need to log in to complete the questionnaire.

□ You can get personalized health insurance counseling at no cost from your local State Health Insurance Assistance Program (SHIP).

□ Once you are enrolled in Medicare, you can no longer contribute to a health savings account (HSA). However, you can still use money from an established HSA to pay for medical expenses until the account is depleted.

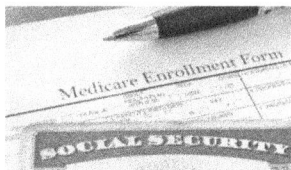

Credit: zimmytws

Checklist: Costs of Medicare Part A

□ If you or your spouse worked at least 10 years in a Medicare taxable job, you will not be charged a premium for Part A coverage.

□ If you paid Medicare taxes for between 30 and 39 quarters (7.5 years to 9.75 years), your Part A premium will be $252.

□ If you paid Medicare taxes for less than 30 quarters, your Part A premium will be $458.

□ Part A premiums may increase by 10% if you didn't enroll in your Initial Enrollment Period. This increase lasts for twice as long as the number of years that you could have been enrolled in Part A but were not.

□ Part A pays for a portion of the services and supplies that Medicare deems medically necessary. If a procedure or treatment is not medically necessary or approved by Medicare, it will not be covered. In addition, if the healthcare facility charges more than Medicare deems reasonable (the

"Medicare-approved amount"), you may be required to pay the amount above the Medicare-approved amount.

☐ If you require inpatient care in an acute care hospital, long-term care hospital, or mental hospital, you will have to pay a $1,408 deductible for each benefit period, $0 co-insurance for each benefit period for days 1–60, $352 co-insurance per day of each benefit period for days 61–90, and $704 co-insurance per each "lifetime reserve day" after day 90 for each benefit period. (Each individual has up to 60 lifetime reserve days they can use over their lifetime.) If you require inpatient hospital care beyond the lifetime reserve days, you will have to pay all costs.

☐ For inpatient hospital care, Medicare will generally not cover private-duty nursing, a private room, television and phone in the room, and personal care items. If you want a private room, you will be responsible for paying the costs associated with that room. However, if a private room is the only room available or offered, then Medicare will pay costs associated with that room.

☐ If you require skilled nursing care in a skilled nursing facility (SNF) for a limited time, you will pay $0 for the first 20 days, $176 for days 21–100, and all costs for days 101 and beyond. However, in order to qualify for these benefits, you must first have a qualified hospital stay of 3 inpatient days. Outpatient days, such as

Credit: James Steidl

18

days spent in the ER for observation, do not count toward the 3 days.

☐ If you are released from the SNF and re-enter the SNF in 30 days or less, you do not need another qualifying hospital stay for Medicare to pay SNF costs. Coverage days begin where the previous stay left off. For example, if you were in the SNF for 15 days on your last stay, your new stay will start on day 16 of coverage.

☐ If you are released from the SNF and re-enter the SNF in 31 to 59 days, you need a new 3-day hospital stay to qualify for Medicare coverage. However, coverage days still begin where the previous stay left off.

☐ If you are released from the SNF and re-enter the SNF after 60 days, you will need a new 3-day hospital stay to qualify for coverage, but the SNF coverage starts over at day 1.

☐ If you need intermittent at-home skilled nursing care or therapy (physical, occupational, speech), Medicare will pay 100% of physician-ordered home healthcare services and 80% of the Medicare-approved amount for medical equipment. However, this does not include 24-hour-a-day at-home care, meals, homemaker services, or personal care; and the individual's condition must be expected to improve over a reasonable period of time. Therefore, individuals with a terminal illness may not be eligible for these benefits.

☐ Medicare Part A covers nursing home costs only if you require skilled nursing care (e.g., changing sterile bandages). Medicare does not generally pay for nursing home care if you only need custodial care (e.g., help with walking, bathing, etc.).

☐ If your doctor certifies that you have six months or less to live, you will be eligible for hospice care coverage under Medicare. You pay $0 for hospice care, but you may need to pay a co-payment of $5 or less for prescription medications that relieve symptoms. Once you are on hospice care, Medicare no longer pays for treatment intended to cure a terminal illness, room and board at long-term care facilities, or care in an emergency room or hospital.

Checklist: Costs of Medicare Part B

☐ The premium for Part B depends on marital status, tax filing status if married, and income range. The standard part B premium is $144.60.

☐ For single individuals with an annual income of $87,000 or less, the Part B premium is $144.60 per month. The premium increases as income increases. The highest rate for single individuals with an annual income greater than or equal to $500,000 or more is $491.60.

☐ Married couples who file taxes jointly have similar premiums to single individuals, but the income amount is greater. For example, if the couple makes $174,000 or less, their premium will be $144.60, and if they make $750,000 or more, their premium will be $491.60.

☐ Married couples who file taxes separately reach the maximum premium ($491.60) with an individual income greater than or equal to $413,000.

☐ If you did not sign up during the Initial Enrollment Period or during a Special Enrollment Period, you may be assessed a late enrollment penalty. The monthly premium may increase by as much as 10%

for every 12-month period that you could have had Part B but did not.

☐ Similar to Part A, Part B coverage only extends to services and supplies that are deemed medically necessary. This includes some preventive services. Examples of covered services include doctor visits, lab tests, surgeries, ambulance services, durable medical equipment, and mental health care.

☐ You will likely pay nothing for most preventive services if you have Part B. Examples of preventive services include an annual wellness visit; vaccines for the flu, pneumonia, and hepatitis B; screenings for cancer, diabetes, depression, sexually transmitted infections, and cardiovascular disease; glaucoma tests; nutrition services; and others.

☐ For most other medical services, you will be responsible for paying 20% of the Medicare-approved amount after you have met your deductible. The Part B deductible is $198 per year.

☐ Providers of some services, such as speech, occupational, and physical therapy, may recommend you receive services more often than Medicare covers or they may recommend services that are not covered. If this occurs, you will be responsible for covering all or some of the cost of these services.

☐ In order for Medicare to cover durable medical equipment, the equipment must be prescribed by a Medicare-approved physician and provided by a Medicare-approved supplier. In addition, Medicare may dictate whether you rent or buy the equipment. Examples of covered medical equipment include blood sugar monitors and test strips, mobility aids (crutches, canes, wheelchairs, walkers), hospital beds, infusion pumps, and oxygen equipment.

☐ For mental health services provided by a hospital outpatient clinic or department, you may have to pay an additional co-payment or co-insurance amount to the hospital.

☐ You may be partially covered for medical expenses associated with a clinical study if you participate in one. If you participate in a clinical trial, discuss costs with both the study facilitators and Medicare to determine which costs will be covered.

Checklist: Basics about Medicare Part C

☐ Medicare Part C plans are offered by private insurance companies rather than the government.

☐ Before enrolling in Part C, you must first enroll in Part A and Part B to confirm eligibility. Then you may choose a Part C plan.

☐ At a minimum, the law requires Part C plans to cover the same services covered by Part A and Part B.

☐ In addition to hospital and medical costs, Medicare Part C may cover extra services that are not covered under Part A and Part B, such as dental, vision, and hearing.

☐ Most Part C plans also offer prescription coverage.

☐ Similar to private insurance plans, Medicare Part C plans usually allow you to choose one primary care provider; your access to other providers and specialists is restricted based on which physicians are in the plan's network. If you use a provider outside the network, you will usually pay more than for services provided by an in-network provider.

☐ If you want to regularly use an out-of-network provider, consider choosing a private fee-for-service plan, which allows you to pay a set fee for each service. However, this may still be more expensive and will likely require extra paperwork.

Checklist: Costs of Medicare Part C

☐ Unlike Part A and Part B, Medicare Part C prices vary based on the provider and plan benefits, similar to private insurance plans. However, the cost generally includes the Part B premium as described above plus a Part C additional premium. The Part C premium varies by plan.

☐ Factors that affect the premium for Medicare Part C include the amount of the deductible, the types of services you sign up for, and the co-payments associated with the plan.

☐ Factors that affect out-of-pocket costs include the amount of the co-payments and deductible, whether the plan pays for the monthly Part B premium, whether you use in-network providers, the yearly out-of-pocket maximum, and others.

Checklist: Basics about Medicare Part D

☐ Medicare offers optional prescription drug coverage to everyone enrolled in Medicare. If you decide not to sign up for Medicare Part D when you are first eligible and you don't have other creditable prescription drug coverage, you will likely pay a late enrollment penalty if you want to enroll later.

☐ Similar to Part C, Part D plans are provided by private insurance companies. These plans add drug coverage for individuals with Medicare Part A and Part B. Different plans vary in premium cost and in the drugs they cover.

☐ Each Part D plan has its own list of covered drugs (called a formulary). Many Medicare drug plans place medications into "tiers" on their formularies. Drugs in each tier have a different cost.

☐ If you have a Medicare Advantage Plan (Part C), you cannot get prescription drug coverage through Part D. Instead, you can add prescription drug coverage directly through your Part C plan. If you want to enroll in Part D, you will be disenrolled from your Part C plan and returned to a regular Part A/Part B plan.

☐ Once you choose a Medicare drug plan, you can apply by enrolling in the Medicare Plan Finder, visiting the plan's website, completing a paper enrollment form, calling the plan, or calling 1-800-MEDICARE (1-800-633-4227).

Checklist: Costs of Medicare Part D

☐ Costs for Part D depend on which private insurance company carries the plan and which insurance plan you choose.

☐ Part D plans usually have a monthly premium. Monthly premiums may be increased if your gross income is above a certain limit based on tax returns two years ago. Therefore, the adjusted premium may change each year depending on your income. Individuals with an income of $87,000 or less will not have to pay this extra

premium. The maximum extra premium is $76.40 per month for individuals with an income equal to or greater than $500,000. This adjusted amount is paid to Medicare, not to the drug plan.

☐ You will be responsible for paying a co-pay or co-insurance for each prescription. This amount will depend on which tier the specific medication is in. Generic drugs are generally in a lower tier than brand-name drugs and thus have a lower co-pay or co-insurance amount.

☐ Medicare Part D only covers select drugs, so you may also be responsible for costs of medications that are not included in Medicare Part D.

☐ Some plans also have a deductible that you will need to pay before the plan begins covering drug costs. The maximum deductible allowed is $435 in 2020.

☐ Prior to 2020, Part D covered up to a specified amount for prescription medications. When this limit was reached, you entered the "donut hole" or coverage gap. While in the donut hole, you had to pay a higher amount for prescription drugs until you reached the out-of-pocket maximum.

☐ In 2020, the donut hole will "close." In other words, once your initial deductible is paid, you will be responsible for 25% of the cost of either generic or brand-name drugs. You will pay this amount until you reach the out-of-pocket maximum and enter catastrophic coverage. The donut hole is expected to remain closed beyond 2020.

☐ Once you have paid the out-of-pocket maximum ($6,350) in one year, including deductibles, co-insurance, and co-payments, you will enter catastrophic coverage. In catastrophic coverage, you will be responsible for only a small co-insurance or co-payment for prescription medications. This amount is equal to about 5% of the cost of your drugs.

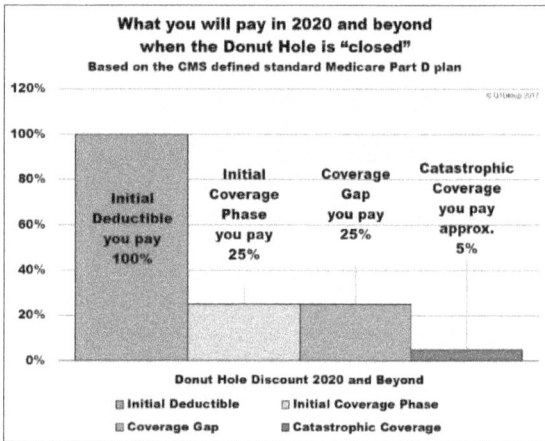

What you will pay in 2020 and beyond when the Donut Hole is "closed"
Based on the CMS defined standard Medicare Part D plan

If you have trouble paying medical costs associated with Medicare, several resources are available to help cover costs such as premiums, deductibles, co-insurance, co-payments, and long-term care. These programs include Medigap insurance, Extra Help, and Medicare Savings Programs. The checklists in the following section provide basic information about each of these programs.

Checklist: Basics about Medicare supplemental insurance (Medigap insurance)

☐ Medigap can help pay some of the healthcare costs that Medicare Part A and Part B don't cover. To be covered, a person must also have Part A and Part B. Medigap insurance is not available to individuals with Medicare Part C.

☐ Similar to Medicare Part C and Part D, Medicare supplemental (Medigap) insurance is sold by private companies. It is not a government program.

☐ A Medigap policy is different from a Medicare Advantage Plan (Part C). Whereas Advantage Plans are an alternative way to get Medicare benefits, Medigap policies only add coverage to a person's Plan A and Plan B benefits.

☐ A Medigap policy only covers one person. Each individual must select and pay for their own Medigap plan.

☐ Each individual is only allowed to select one Medigap plan. Insurance companies are not allowed to sell more than one Medigap plan to an individual.

☐ Insurance companies are not allowed to sell a Medigap policy to individuals who participate in the Medicare Savings Program or have coverage through Medicaid.

☐ Individuals who have Medicare coverage based on a disability who are under the age of 65 may not be eligible for Medigap insurance.

☐ When purchasing a Medigap policy, first decide which benefits you need, then decide which of

Medigap plans A–N best meet that need. These plans are standardized (except in Massachusetts, Minnesota, and Wisconsin), so each letter plan should offer the same benefits in different states and through different insurance companies.

☐ Each Medigap plan offers a different set of benefits, filling different gaps in Medicare Part A and Part B. Depending on the gaps that most affect you, one Medigap plan may be more beneficial than another plan.

☐ Depending on the Medigap plan selected, the plan may cover all or part of your Part A and Part B deductible, Part A and Part B co-insurance and co-payments, costs above the Medicare-approved amount, and inpatient hospital costs above the Medicare maximum.

☐ Medigap policies generally don't cover long-term care, vision or dental care, hearing aids, eyeglasses, private-duty nursing, or prescription drug costs.

☐ When choosing a Medigap plan, take time to think about what type of coverage you might need in the future. Unless your coverage ends for a variety of reasons (such as the insurance company going out of business, the plan no longer being offered, or moving out of the coverage area for the plan), the options for switching Medigap plans are limited. Therefore, you need to select the policy that will best fit your needs long term.

☐ Once you have selected the Medigap plan that is right for you, you can view companies that offer that plan and get contact information for each company.

- Most insurance companies only sell some of the Medigap plans, so make sure the company you contact sells the plan you need. Carefully read any information you are given about the policy and its benefits and costs, and don't be afraid to ask questions if you don't understand something.

- Medigap premiums must be paid in addition to Part A and Part B premiums. Different states and different insurance companies offer different premium rates for the same plan with the same benefits, so it is important to shop around before purchasing a policy.

- Make sure you understand the insurance company's pricing system for premiums. Some companies use community-rated pricing, in which everyone pays the same amount regardless of age; premium increases are based on inflation, not on age. Some companies use issue-age-rated pricing, in which the premium cost depends on your age when you initially purchase the plan; additional premium increases are based on inflation, not on age. Some companies use attained-age-rated pricing, in which the premium increases each year based on age.

- Each individual has a one-time grace period for enrolling in a Medigap plan. This grace period starts on the first day of the month in which the individual is both 65 years old or older AND is enrolled in Medicare Part B. This open enrollment period extends for a total of 6 months.

- During the open enrollment period, insurance companies cannot deny coverage to you for a pre-existing condition. If you do not enroll in a Medigap plan during this grace period, insurance companies have the right to deny you coverage or to charge more for the policy based on your health status.

☐ Although insurance companies cannot deny coverage to an individual during the open enrollment period due to pre-existing health conditions, they can delay coverage of those pre-existing conditions. This waiting period is generally six months before they will begin to cover medical expenses related to the pre-existing condition. However, Medicare Part A and Part B will still cover expenses related to the pre-existing condition during this waiting period.

☐ Once you have a Medigap policy, the insurance company cannot cancel the policy based on health conditions as long as you continue to pay the premiums.

Applying for Medigap insurance can be overwhelming due to the number of choices that must be made. AARP and SHIP (State Health Insurance Assistance Program) both provide assistance in choosing a Medigap plan. If you don't understand your options, resources are available to help answer your questions and walk you through your choices.

Checklist: Basics about Extra Help

☐ Just as Medigap helps cover the gap for Medicare Part A and Part B, Extra Help helps cover the gap for Medicare Part D for eligible individuals.

☐ Extra Help assists individuals in paying for Medicare Part D premiums, deductibles, and co-insurance or co-payments.

☐ You must provide documentation of financial hardship to qualify for Extra Help (assets of $14,390 or less for a single individual or combined assets of $28,720 or less for a married couple living together).

☐ When determining eligibility, cash accounts, stocks, and bonds count as assets. A primary home, one vehicle, personal belongings, and some money set aside for burial expenses are not counted as assets.

☐ Because eligibility depends on assets and income, your eligibility status may change each year if your assets and/or income change.

☐ If you are covered by Medicaid or Supplemental Security Income (SSI), you are automatically eligible for Extra Help.

☐ If you are not eligible for Extra Help, you can still purchase a Medicare Part D prescription drug plan.

☐ In most states, individuals enrolled in Extra Help will pay no more than $3.60 for each generic medication and $8.95 for each brand-name medication that is covered by Medicare. These cheaper medication costs save individuals an average of $4,900 per year, but you will still have to pay regular price for medications not covered by Medicare.

☐ You can apply for Extra Help by going to the Social Security website or calling Social Security at 1-800-772-1213.

Checklist: Basics about Medicare Savings Programs

☐ Medicare Savings Programs help individuals with low income and assets pay their Part A premium,

Part B premium, and/or Part A and Part B deductibles, co-insurance, and co-payments.

☐ The four Medicare Savings Programs have different eligibility requirements and benefits: Qualified Medicare Beneficiary (QMB) Program, Specified Low-Income Medicare Beneficiary (SLMB) Program, Qualifying Individual (QI) Program, and Qualified Disabled and Working Individuals (QDWI) Program.

☐ The QMB Program helps pay for Part A and Part B premiums, deductibles, co-insurance, and co-payments for individuals with a monthly income of no more than $1,061 (in 2019) and assets of no more than $7,730 and couples with a monthly income of no more than $1,430 and assets of no more than $11,600.

☐ The SLMB Program helps pay Part B premiums for individuals with a monthly income of no more than $1,269 (in 2019) and assets of no more than $7,730 and couples with a monthly income of no more than $1,711 and assets of no more than $11,600.

☐ The QI Program helps pay Part B premiums for individuals with a monthly income of no more than $1,426 (in 2019) and assets of no more than $7,730 and couples with a monthly income of no more than $1,923 and assets of no more than $11,600. If you qualify for the QI program, you must apply every year, and applications are granted on a first-come, first-served basis. Priority is given to people who received QI benefits the previous year. Individuals receiving Medicaid benefits cannot receive QI benefits.

☐ The QDWI Program helps pay Part A premiums for individuals with a monthly income of no more

than $4,249 (in 2019) and assets of no more than
$4,000 and couples with a monthly income of no
more than $5,722 and assets of no more than
$6,000. This program is for working individuals
who are disabled and are under the age of 65, who
lost their premium-free Part A when they went
back to work, and who aren't getting state
medical assistance.

☐ Individuals who qualify for Extra Help should
apply for a Medicare Savings Program, and
individuals who qualify for a Medicare Savings
Program are automatically eligible for Extra Help.

☐ Similar to Extra Help, countable assets include cash
accounts, stocks, and bonds. Countable assets do
not include a primary residence, one vehicle,
personal belongings, and some money set aside for
burial expenses. Some states count assets and
income differently, so if you need help paying for
your Medicare expenses, apply for a Medicare
Savings Program to determine your eligibility.

☐ To apply for a Medicare Savings Program, call your
state Medicaid program.

Medicaid

Individuals on Medicare and other supplemental
insurance programs as well as individuals under the age of
65 may be eligible for
Medicaid if they meet certain
income and/or asset
requirements. Medicaid is a
government-funded health
insurance program for low-
income individuals and
families who meet certain

Credit: txking

33

income and asset requirements. Individuals who cannot pay for traditional health insurance can apply for help from Medicaid to pay their medical and hospital bills. Individuals who qualify may also receive help with long-term care costs, but the requirements for these benefits are very strict. Determining eligibility and applying for Medicaid may seem complicated, but finding out whether you qualify for benefits can pay off both immediately and in the long run.

Checklist: Basics about Medicaid

- ☐ Medicaid is a health insurance program for individuals with low income and few assets.

- ☐ Medicaid is funded jointly by the federal and state governments and is administered by state governments. Therefore, different states may have different services and requirements for their Medicaid program. However, each state must provide at least minimum benefits as outlined by the federal government.

- ☐ Similar to Medicare, Medicaid provides hospital and medical insurance for qualified individuals. However, individuals with full Medicaid benefits also receive a wider array of services, including long-term nursing care. Some states may also cover dental, eye, and hearing services.

- ☐ If you are diagnosed with a terminal illness at a young age, have to quit your job, and still have children under the age of 21 at home, the children may be eligible for health insurance through CHIP (Children's Health Insurance Program) depending on family income requirements, even if the adults in the family are not eligible. CHIP is essentially the children's division of Medicaid.

□ You can enroll in Medicaid at any point during the year. To determine if you may be eligible for Medicaid, use Medicaid's online screener.

□ If you qualify for Medicaid, you have two options for applying. The first option is to apply directly to your state agency after determining eligibility online. With this option, coverage can begin immediately. The other option is to fill out a Marketplace application online. These applications are open only from the middle of November through the middle of February.

Checklist: Medicaid regulations for individuals under age 65

□ For individuals under the age of 65, the sole determining factor for basic Medicaid eligibility is the individual or family's modified adjusted gross income, or MAGI. To qualify for Medicaid, the individual or family's MAGI must be under a certain percentage of the federal poverty level (FPL), usually 138% of the FPL or less. The percentage varies by state. In 2019, the FPL for one individual is an annual income of $12,490, whereas the FPL for a family of four is an annual income of $25,750. In states with expanded Medicaid coverage, having an income below the FPL is the only requirement, whereas in other states eligibility requirements vary by state, with qualification for Medicaid based on income, household size, disability, family status, and other factors.

□ Because some states provide Medicaid coverage for individuals with incomes above 138% of the poverty level, they can choose to require monthly premiums, co-payments, co-insurance, and deductibles for these higher-income individuals. However, these costs are usually minimal compared to private insurance plans.

☐ Individuals who are under the age of 65 who do not meet income requirements for Medicaid may still be eligible for Medicaid in their state if they are deemed "medically needy."

☐ Medically needy individuals can qualify for Medicaid during the spend-down period specified by their state depending on their medical bills. If their medical bills are high enough to reduce the individual's usable income to below the income amount allowed by their state, they are eligible to qualify for Medicaid through the Excess Income Program.

☐ In the Excess Income Program, individuals can submit medical bills to Medicaid to become eligible for Medicaid. The amount of medical bills that must be submitted depends on the individual's income level. For example, an individual who has a monthly income that is $50 above their MAGI limit will have to prove that they have $50 or more in medical bills for that month. Once they prove they have hit that limit, they are eligible for Medicaid benefits for their remaining medical expenses for that month. Some states may also require an asset limit before a medically needy individual is eligible for Medicaid.

☐ Paid medical bills can be applied to the excess income for up to six months, depending on the spend-down period for your state. For example, if the spend-down period in your state is six months and you have excess income of $50 and you paid $25 in medical bills in July and $25 in medical bills in August, you can combine those two months to be eligible for Medicaid for the remainder of August or for any month through December. Similarly, if you paid $200 in medical bills in September with excess income of $50 per month, you will qualify for Medicaid for any four-month time span between September and February.

☐ In states that require an individual to submit receipts or bills to Medicaid to show monthly expenses, unpaid medical bills can be applied to meet the excess income requirement in any month as long as the bills are still viable (i.e., the medical facility still expects payment). If using unpaid medical bills to qualify for Medicaid, Medicaid will not pay the qualifying bills. They will cover any bills in addition to those qualifying bills, similar to a deductible.

☐ When using medical bills to spend down excess income to qualify for Medicaid, medical bills can only be used once. You cannot use both an unpaid bill and proof of payment for that same bill to qualify for Medicaid in two different months.

☐ Bills that can be used to help spend down excess income include health insurance premiums, deductibles, co-insurance or co-payments, and other medical expenses.

☐ If you want to have consistent Medicaid coverage, some states allow you to pay Medicaid your excess income each month, similar to an insurance premium. You will then be eligible to receive Medicaid benefits.

☐ Some states require that medically needy individuals fulfill their excess income spend-down for multiple months before they will cover inpatient hospital care. For example, if you have

$50 in excess monthly income and your state requires a spend-down of 6 months, you would have to accumulate $300 in in-patient hospital bills before Medicaid coverage of in-patient hospital costs would begin.

Checklist: Medicaid regulations for individuals over age 65 (dual-eligible)

☐ Dual-eligible individuals qualify for both Medicare and Medicaid. Generally, these are individuals over the age of 65 with low income and few assets. However, individuals who qualify for Medicare based on a disability or end-stage renal disease may be under the age of 65.

☐ For dual-eligible individuals, the MAGI rule for Medicaid eligibility does not apply. Dual-eligible individuals must meet both income and asset requirements to qualify for Medicaid.

☐ To qualify for full Medicaid benefits, including long-term care coverage, individuals must meet asset and income requirements as determined by the state. For more on these requirements, see Checklist: Medicaid and long-term nursing care coverage.

☐ Individuals who do not meet the requirements for full Medicaid benefits may be eligible for Medicaid support through a Medicare Savings Program with its established income and asset requirements. These individuals may receive help paying for their Part A, Part B, and Part D premiums, deductibles, co-insurance, and co-payments but not long-term care costs.

☐ In addition to services covered through Medicare, individuals who qualify for Medicaid may have access to additional benefits above the normal Medicare benefits, including prescription drug coverage, eyeglasses, and hearing aids.

Checklist: Medicaid and long-term nursing care

☐ For all individuals who require nursing home care (both MAGI-eligible and dual-eligible), Medicaid has strict income and asset requirements before they will begin to pay for long-term care.

☐ Generally, income requirements are similar to MAGI rules (138% of FPL or less). Asset requirements are usually $2,000 or less of accumulated assets for an individual or $3,000 or less for a couple. States with expanded Medicaid coverage have no asset requirements. These requirements vary widely among states, so check with your local Social Security office to determine the requirements for your state.

☐ Assets that count toward the asset limit include cash accounts, investments, some real estate, and some retirement accounts. Assets that generally do not count toward asset limits include the primary home, one vehicle, and personal possessions. Other assets and income that count toward the asset limit may vary by state.

☐ In order to qualify for full Medicaid nursing home coverage, some individuals may need to "spend down" their income and assets.

☐ The income spend-down is similar to the spend-down for medically needy individuals. You will be required to use your excess monthly income to pay for medical and long-term care costs, and once that amount is spent, Medicaid will cover the rest of the costs.

☐ Spend-down of assets is strictly regulated by Medicaid. Individuals are allowed to spend down their assets for normal living and medical expenses without incurring a Medicaid penalty. They are not allowed to spend down assets simply by giving away their assets to others. Assets that are given away will be subject to a 5-year "look back" period.

☐ During the look back period, if the Medicaid applicant has given away assets to children, grandchildren, or others, these gifts can be counted against them for Medicaid eligibility. For example, if you gave each of three grandchildren $10,000 two years ago and you apply for Medicaid now, you will incur a $30,000 penalty for long-term care coverage if you are otherwise eligible to receive Medicaid.

☐ Your Medicaid penalty, if you have one, will be assessed based on your monthly expenses. For example, if you have a Medicaid penalty of $30,000 and expect to need $5,000 per month for long-term nursing care, Medicaid will not pay for the first 6 months ($30,000/$5,000 = 6).

☐ Asset transfers that do not incur a Medicaid penalty include transfers to a spouse up to a certain limit, a child who is blind or has a disability, a trust for the benefit of a child who is blind or has a disability, or a trust for the sole benefit of an individual under age 65 who has a disability.

☐ If you incur a penalty period, the penalty period will not apply until you move into a nursing home, have spent down your assets based on Medicaid stipulations, apply for Medicaid, and are approved for coverage. Once all these conditions are met, the penalty period will start; once the penalty period is over, Medicaid will pay nursing home costs.

☐ Because medical expenses can be severe, especially long-term nursing care expenses, costing anywhere from $4,471 per month for a semi-private room in Oklahoma to an astonishing $24,335 per month for a private in room in Alaska (2019 averages), Medicaid allows some individuals needing this level of care to be eligible for Medicaid at a higher income or asset level if paying for these services out-of-pocket causes undue hardship for their spouse. This is called spousal impoverishment.

☐ Under Medicaid's spousal impoverishment provisions, a certain amount of a couple's combined resources are protected for use by the spouse still living in the community. Depending on the couple's needs, the monthly maintenance needs allowance for the spouse in the community is between $2,113.75 (except for Alaska, $2,641.25, and Hawaii, $2,432.50) and $3,160.50; the monthly housing allowance is $634.13 for all states except Alaska ($792.38) and Hawaii ($729.75); the available assets are between $25,284 and $126,420; and the home equity limits are between $585,000 and $878,000. Any shared income or resources above these limits must be used to pay for long-term care before Medicaid begins to pay for care (i.e., the couple must spend down their excess income and assets).

☐ If you have a terminal illness and are in the nursing home and your spouse does not have enough personal income to meet their monthly maintenance needs allowance, you can transfer assets to your spouse up to the allowance amount rather than using that income to pay for nursing home costs.

☐ Individuals with Medicaid coverage who need long-term nursing care may have limited choices for which nursing home they can use. Specifically, Medicaid will only cover services provided in a nursing home that is licensed and certified as a Medicaid Nursing Facility. However, if you are already in a nursing home when you become eligible for Medicaid, Medicaid and the nursing facility usually do not require you to move to a new facility if your current facility is not a certified Medicaid Nursing Facility.

☐ If you have Medicaid coverage and you are not yet in a nursing home, you may be placed on a waiting list for a Medicaid Nursing Facility, because the number of "Medicaid beds" might be limited in your preferred nursing home.

Checklist: Medicaid Estate Recovery program

☐ If you receive Medicaid coverage for long-term nursing home care and are over the age of 55, your estate may be subject to the Medicaid Estate Recovery program after your death.

☐ The Medicaid Estate Recovery program allows Medicaid to make claims on your possessions to recover the cost of your care for nursing facility services, home and community-based services, and related hospital and prescription drug services. About half of the states recover payments for all Medicaid services, not just long-term care services.

☐ Your remaining debts (mortgage, credit card debt, unpaid utility bills, etc.) receive higher priority for payment than the Medicaid Estate Recovery program. Medicaid can only claim what's left of the estate after these debts have been paid.

☐ Medicaid can only claim up to the amount that they paid out for services. If your estate has greater value than your Medicaid claims, Medicaid cannot recover the entirety of your estate.

☐ In some states, possessions that pass to a beneficiary without going through probate court may be exempt from recovery by Medicaid. This includes jointly-held assets, assets in a living trust, or life estates. However, different states have different rules about the definition of "estate" and whether non-probate assets are recoverable, so check with your state policy to determine which assets may be subject to Medicaid recovery.

☐ Because of the Medicaid asset restrictions, the most substantial asset that you are likely to own at the time of your death is your primary residence.

☐ Medicaid may require that your home be sold for repayment of Medicaid benefits. However, the home is protected if a spouse, child under the age of 21, child of any age who is blind or has a disability, or sibling with equity interest in the home still lives in the home. Property may also be protected if it is income-generating for heirs, such as a farm, rental property, or family business. However, if the surviving spouse is the only one with a claim to the home, Medicaid may come back after the spouse's death and recover the cost of the home.

☐ Medicaid is also allowed to place a lien on your home or other real estate so that when the real estate is sold before or after your death, Medicaid can collect repayment from the proceeds of the sale.

☐ Medicaid may waive their right to recovery if recovery of your estate may cause undue hardship for your heirs. This undue hardship is defined differently in each state, and heirs often have to request the waiver during the probate process.

☐ Family members should not be expected to repay Medicaid with their own money unless they received assets from your estate. Then, only assets received from the estate are subject to recovery. Other personal possessions, assets, and income are not subject to recovery. However, if Medicaid has placed a lien on your home and your family wants to keep the home in the family, they may have to repay Medicaid for the cost of the house from their personal funds.

As you can see, government health insurance regulations and eligibility requirements are very confusing, and many programs differ depending on state regulations. If you think you may qualify for one of these programs, call your local Social Security office to discuss your eligibility and to sign up for each program.

Another program run through Medicaid that may benefit you is PACE (Program of All-Inclusive Care for the Elderly). This program is designed to help you live in the community as long as possible rather than having to live in an assisted living or long-term care facility. PACE programs are only available in limited areas, so check with your local Medicaid office to determine if a PACE program is available in your area.

Checklist: Basics about PACE (Program of All-Inclusive Care for the Elderly)

☐ PACE is a healthcare program that provides comprehensive care to enable individuals to meet their healthcare needs in the community rather than in a long-term care facility.

☐ To be eligible for PACE, you must be 55 years old or older, live in a PACE service area, need nursing home-level care, and be able to live safely in the community with the help of PACE.

☐ Individuals enrolled in PACE receive care and services in the home, the community, and/or the local PACE center. The PACE center has local contracts with physicians and other providers to deliver the care that is needed. Individuals in the PACE program are required to use participating PACE providers.

☐ Each individual is cared for by a small number of people, so the caregivers really get to know the individual and their needs.

☐ PACE covers services including adult day care, dentistry, emergency services, home care, hospital care, preventive care, meals, medical specialty services, nursing home care, nutritional counseling, occupational and physical therapy, prescription drugs, transportation to the PACE center as needed, and respite care for caregivers.

☐ If you are enrolled in PACE, you do not need to enroll in Medicare Part D. All of your prescription drugs will be provided through PACE.

□ The premium for PACE depends on your financial situation. If you are enrolled in Medicaid, you won't have to pay a monthly premium. If you are not eligible for Medicaid but you have Medicare, you will be charged a monthly premium to cover long-term care and the Part D benefit. If you do not have Medicare or Medicaid, you can pay for PACE privately.

□ Once enrolled in PACE, the premium will not increase even if you need more care and services.

□ Individuals who are enrolled in PACE do not pay any deductibles or co-payments for any drug, service, or care provided by the PACE healthcare team. Care provided by individuals outside the PACE team will need to be paid by the individual or other insurance policy.

□ Individuals enrolled in PACE can leave the program at any time.

□ To apply, contact your state Medicaid office.

Long-Term Care Insurance

Long-term care insurance is vital to paying for living costs associated with chronic terminal illness, including at-home medical care, assisted living, and memory care unit costs. A few basic concepts related to the cost of long-term care insurance are included in the checklist below.

Checklist: Basics about long-term care insurance costs

□ Premiums for long-term care insurance depend on a person's health and age, the policy's waiting period and benefit period, and the amount of the daily benefit, among other factors. Married couples may receive a discount.

☐ The waiting period is the amount of time that must pass between when the individual is eligible for benefits and when the insurance begins paying. This is typically 0, 30, 60, or 90 days. In addition, many insurance companies require that the waiting period include only days that care is received. For example, if you receive at-home care five days per week and the policy has a 30-day waiting period, benefits will begin after six weeks.

☐ Eligibility for benefits usually depends on your inability to perform a certain number of activities of daily living (ADLs), such as bathing, dressing, eating, or toileting. Most policies state that you must be unable to perform two ADLs before eligibility occurs. This is called a benefit trigger.

☐ The benefit period is the minimum amount of time that the policy will cover your expenses. This is typically 1, 2, 3, or 5 years.

☐ The daily benefit is the maximum costs that the policy will cover per day: for example, $150. Costs above this per day must be paid by the policy holder. The daily benefit is often applied in full for nursing home care, but the insurance company may pay only a portion (usually 50% to 75%) of the daily benefit for other services, such as assisted living or at-home care.

☐ As an example, let's say that you have a long-term care insurance policy with a five-year benefit period and a daily benefit of $150 per day. This policy will cover a total of $273,750 (365 days × 5 years × $150/day) in long-term care expenses over five or more years, depending on how long it takes to accrue that level of expenses.

☐ Once you reach the maximum benefit under your chosen plan, you will no longer be eligible for payment of long-term care costs under your insurance policy. Therefore, it is vital that you select adequate benefits when you purchase your policy.

☐ Annual premiums can vary based on a number of factors, including age and marital status, place of residence, and whether the policy has inflation protection. For example, for a single male age 55 with a three-year plan ($164,000 initial pool of benefits growing 3 percent compounded annually), the 2019 average annual premium would be $2,050. For a single female age 55 with the same policy, the 2019 average annual premium would be $2,700. Premium costs may fall above or below this for policies with different benefit packages.

☐ If you have already been diagnosed with a chronic terminal illness before you purchase long-term care insurance, you may be denied coverage if a medical examination is required. The premiums may also be cost prohibitive.

Another option for long-term care insurance is to purchase a policy through the state's Partnership program. These programs offer asset protection as well as payment of long-term care costs. However, not all states have a participating Partnership program. Some basics related to the costs of Partnership programs are included in the following checklist.

Checklist: Basics about Partnership programs

☐ Although they have the additional benefit of asset protection, most state-sponsored long-term care Partnership plans have similar premiums as an equivalent private long-term care insurance policy. However, this may not be true in all states.

☐ Asset protection means that a certain amount of the policy holder's personal assets will be protected from the Medicaid asset requirement. To see more about Medicaid asset requirements, see Checklist: Medicaid and long-term nursing care coverage.

☐ If you have a Partnership plan with asset protection, you can increase the amount of countable assets you are allowed to have for Medicaid eligibility. This asset protection is associated with the individual's coverage under the Partnership plan.

☐ For example, if you have a three-year benefit period with a $200 daily benefit, you will have benefits and asset protection equaling $219,000 (365 days × 3 years × $200/day). Therefore, if your basic Medicaid asset requirement is less than $2,000, you will be eligible for Medicaid if you have less than $221,000 ($219,000 + $2,000) in total countable assets when the benefits of the Partnership plan are exhausted.

☐ Even with asset protection, individuals with monthly income above the Medicaid requirements will be required to use their excess income to pay for care in order to qualify for Medicaid. This is called spending down your income.

☐ For wealthy individuals, some states offer a "total" asset protection plan. With a Partnership plan that contains total asset protection, all of your assets will be protected if you exhaust your long-term care insurance benefits and need to apply for Medicaid. These plans are usually much more expensive than other Partnership plans.

☐ Most states that participate in Partnership programs have reciprocity. This means that if you purchase your Partnership policy in one state and later move to another state, your new state will honor your Partnership policy, including asset protection. Currently, California is the only state that participates in the Partnership program that does not have reciprocity. However, nine additional states that do not sell Partnership long-term policies also will not honor Partnership policies from other states.

Disability Insurance

If you are working at the time of a debilitating accident or diagnosis of a terminal illness, you may have disability insurance either through your employer or through private insurance. Depending on whether you had to quit your job because of the effects of the accident or illness and/or the stage of the illness, disability insurance may provide a source of income for you. Note that the amount you will receive from your disability insurance payouts is often dependent on your salary at the time of disability, so you should not continue to pay premiums for disability insurance if you are no longer working and receiving a salary. The checklist below contains basic information about receiving benefits from disability insurance.

Checklist: Basics about private disability insurance

☐ Private disability income insurance provides income for a person who must stop working due to injury or illness. However, some disability insurance policies only cover accidental injury and not illness, so make sure you check your policy to see if you qualify for benefits.

☐ Some disability insurance policies provided by an employer only cover disability due to on-the-job injuries. Therefore, if you have a terminal illness, you would not qualify to receive benefits from this type of policy.

☐ Disability insurance policies can provide coverage for short-term disability or long-term disability.

☐ For both types of disability insurance, you must meet disability requirements before your elimination period can begin, and then the elimination period must end before you begin receiving benefits.

☐ If you have short-term disability insurance, the elimination period is usually between 0 and 90 days. Short-term disability policies usually provide no more than two years of benefits.

☐ If you have long-term disability insurance, the elimination period is usually between 90 and 365 days, and the insurance may pay benefits from 2 years up to the time you reach the age of 67, depending on the policy you selected.

☐ Policies paid for by employers generally provide 60 to 80 percent of the covered person's gross income. These benefits are taxed.

- [ ] If you bought a personal disability income policy (as opposed to a policy provided by an employer), the benefits will be paid out at the level you chose. These benefits are not taxed.

- [ ] Most insurance companies will waive the premium once you begin collecting payouts from the policy. If the company is still expecting premium payments after benefits begin, call the company to see if they will waive those costs.

Life Insurance

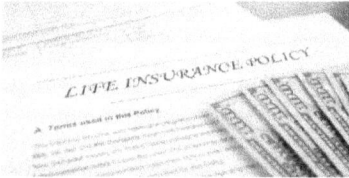

Credit: zimmytws

If you have a short-term need for cash to pay for healthcare costs, a life insurance policy can provide a valuable source of income. However, using life insurance for cash comes with many drawbacks, from insurance company penalties and fees to a reduction in the value of the policy. In addition, you can only borrow from permanent or whole life insurance, not term life insurance. This checklist outlines the four major methods of using an insurance policy for cash: making a withdrawal, taking a loan, surrendering the policy, and making a viatical (or life) settlement. Before taking any of these steps, be sure to talk to an insurance advisor.

Checklist: Basics about borrowing from a life insurance policy

- [ ] **Withdrawal.** Typically, you will be able to withdraw cash you have paid into the policy over time. If taken in small amounts, these withdrawals are not taxable. Drawbacks of withdrawals include reduction in the value of the policy's death or survivor benefit (i.e., the amount survivors will receive), the possibility of increased income taxes, and the possibility of increased insurance premiums to maintain the same death benefit.

☐ **Loan.** If you have permanent, or whole, life insurance, you can borrow some of the money you have paid into it over time. The major drawback of loans is that the value of the death benefit will be reduced if you do not pay back the loan by returning money to the policy. Even if you don't care about replacing the money borrowed from the policy, you will owe annual interest on the loan. If you don't pay back the interest, the interest will start to compound—you will end up paying interest on your interest.

☐ **Surrender.** You can cancel your policy and gain a large amount of cash from the surrender. Drawbacks of surrendering a policy include potentially hefty surrender fees, income taxation, and loss of the policy's death benefit. In addition, a large cash inflow may cause you to become ineligible for Medicaid and Medicare supplemental plans such as Extra Help and Medicare Savings Programs.

☐ **Viatical (life) settlement.** In this situation, the company that provides the viatical settlement buys the insurance policy in exchange for monthly, tax-free cash payments. This option is generally reserved for people with a life expectancy of 5 years or fewer. When you make a viatical settlement, the company becomes the beneficiary of the insurance policy. Your original beneficiaries, such as your spouse or children, will not be paid upon your death.

Chapter 3:
Personal Finances

All medical expenses that are not covered by private or public health insurance will need to be paid out of your personal finances. These finances include any form of income, such as retirement accounts, Social Security, or veteran's benefits, and any form of savings, including cash accounts and investments. The following sections will describe each of these types of income and savings.

Personal Wealth

If you are anticipating medical expenses—particularly in your retirement years—it is essential that you understand your financial resources so you understand what services you are eligible for and can afford. By understanding your resources, you can make sure your bills are paid while protecting your assets as much as possible.

Checklist: Financial resources that can help you pay for healthcare

☐ **Cash accounts.** Checking accounts, savings accounts, certificates of deposit, money market accounts, and other cash accounts can help pay for medical expenses. Many cash accounts provide minimal interest in addition to the funds you deposit.

☐ **Retirement plans**. For retirees, former employers' pension plans or personal retirement accounts may provide a regular source of income.

☐ **Investments.** Investments in bonds, stocks, and mutual funds can provide you with a steady or lump-sum source of income. Income can be in the form of interest, dividends, or the sale price of the investment. Other types of investments are available, but they are for more advanced investors. If you have more complex investments, you may need to discuss your portfolio with a financial advisor or investment banker.

☐ **Social Security.** Social Security retirement benefits, disability benefits, and Supplemental Security Income (SSI) provide monthly income for many retirees and other individuals with chronic terminal illness.

☐ **Veterans Benefits.** If you were in the armed services, you can receive a range of benefits from the U.S. Department of Veterans Affairs.

☐ **Annuities.** An annuity is a contractual financial investment purchased through an insurance company to provide a steady source of income for either a set period of time or for the rest of your life. If you purchased a fixed annuity, the amount of each payment will never vary. If you purchased a variable annuity, the amount of each payment will vary with the value of the annuity's underlying investments. Annuities often have high expenses and large penalties for early withdrawal, so make sure you understand the rules and regulations associated with the annuity before purchase.

☐ **Rental income.** If you own property that you rent or lease, rent payments are a reliable income stream.

☐ **Business income.** If you own a business, you may receive income from the business or you may sell the business to obtain a lump sum of cash that can be used to pay expenses.

☐ **Personal property.** Alternative investments such as real estate, vehicles, jewelry, art, or collectibles can be liquidated to cover care costs.

☐ **Trusts.** You may be the beneficiary of a trust set up by your parents, grandparents, or spouse. Any income or resources from the trust can be used to help pay for medical expenses according to the trust's stipulations.

In the event of a terminal illness, both medical and non-medical expenses can greatly erode your wealth. You may choose to spend all of your assets to pay for your care and qualify for

Credit: Syda Productions

Medicaid. However, if you wish to protect your savings and resources for your descendants' inheritance, the techniques in the checklist below may be beneficial.

Checklist: How to protect your finances

☐ Talk to a qualified financial advisor or attorney for legal advice about protecting your finances. If you've received a diagnosis of a terminal illness, this should be done as soon as possible while you still have the ability to make competent decisions.

☐ Create a durable power of attorney for finances to name a trusted person or group of people to make financial decisions for you while you are alive. This helps protect you from unnecessary spending and scams should you no longer have the mental capacity to make good financial decisions. You must choose your own power of attorney and be legally competent to sign documents, so this should also be done as soon as possible following diagnosis of a terminal illness.

☐ Be aware of common financial scams and types of identity theft, and take action to prevent yourself from becoming a target.

☐ Limit marketing materials that come to your home so you are not tempted to make out-of-the-ordinary, expensive, or unnecessary purchases. Similarly, post a No Soliciting sign on your door.

☐ Organize and protect your financial documents by informing your durable power of attorney where your bank, Social Security, pension, and personal papers are. Store your impossible-to-replace documents, including birth certificates, property deeds, and vehicle titles, in a safe place. If you store them at home, keep these documents in a fireproof and waterproof container. If you store them in a safe deposit box, make sure your durable power of attorney for finances is listed as a co-signee on the box.

☐ Make and stick to a budget. With the added expense of paying for care, a budget is essential for managing your finances if you have a chronic terminal illness.

☐ Pay bills on time to avoid the late fees associated with nonpayment.

☐ Consider switching to online banking and bill paying to prevent mistakes and save money. You'll have access to more information if you bank electronically, and you'll be able to schedule payments automatically and monitor account balances in real time.

☐ Talk to your banking or credit institution to set up a method to protect against overdraft charges and large credit card bills. Banks often allow checking and savings accounts to be linked to prevent overdraft fees, and setting a low spending limit on credit cards can help prevent large credit card bills.

☐ Resist the urge to borrow an "advance" on your future pension, Social Security, or other retirement income. Borrowing from these sources generally involves costly fees and interest.

☐ If possible, don't make early withdrawals from term accounts because doing so can lead to costly fees. These accounts include certificates of deposit (CDs), some investments, and retirement accounts.

☐ Use credit cards cautiously because credit card debt comes with high interest rates and can be difficult to repay later. Ideally, you should only use credit cards if you can completely pay off the balance on the card each month to avoid interest and late fees.

☐ Review your credit reports for errors. A credit report that is free of errors can make it easier to buy insurance and borrow money.

Credit: danielfela

☐ Do not sell your home, especially if a spouse, child under the age of 21, adult child with a disability, or caregiver sibling is still living in the house. An individual's primary residence is exempt from Medicaid asset requirements. If you sell your home and have a windfall of cash, it may cause you to lose eligibility for Medicaid and other programs with asset restrictions. For more about protecting your home, see the following checklist.

☐ Avoid a reverse mortgage if possible. A reverse mortgage is essentially a loan with your house as collateral. The money is paid to you in monthly cash payments that can be used for your care and living expenses. Upon your death, the bank sells the house to recover their investment.

☐ When applying for Medicaid for nursing home care benefits, invoke the spousal impoverishment provisions if your spouse is still living in the community.

☐ If possible, purchase long-term care insurance through a state Partnership program. This allows you to protect your assets up to the amount of your insurance benefits.

☐ If you are paying for banking services, consider switching your accounts to a bank with no account fees.

☐ Prepare for the transfer of financial responsibility and assets by communicating with your durable power of attorney about relevant financial documents and the structure of your finances.

☐ Determine a method of transferring wealth before you are no longer capable of making financial decisions. Typical ways to transfer wealth include gifting assets, selling possessions for a reduced price, and paying for a family member to provide care services.

☐ If you want to transfer wealth by gifting assets or selling them for less than their market value, you should do this as soon as possible. If you gift assets within five years of needing Medicaid to help pay for long-term nursing care, you will be penalized. However, if you give away assets early so the gifts are beyond the look-back period, you will not be penalized by Medicaid. Large gifts may incur gift taxes, so consider the effect of taxes on you and the recipient before giving cash or other assets as a gift.

☐ If a family member is providing caregiving services for you, consider drawing up a caregiver payment agreement to pay the individual for their caregiving services. This may be especially helpful for the family member if they had to quit their job to provide caregiving services for you. Paying a family member for caregiving services helps legitimately transfer wealth and spend down your assets without incurring a Medicaid penalty. However, make sure you and the family member draw up a written, legal agreement to prove to Medicaid that the payments are legitimate. Remember that the family member will be required to pay income taxes on this money, similar to a regular job.

☐ Consider establishing a trust as a way of transferring wealth. In particular, an irrevocable trust can be established for your life insurance policy to ensure that the beneficiaries receive payment after your death. An irrevocable trust is no longer considered the possession of the individual but rather a possession of the beneficiaries. Other types of trusts may also be beneficial.

☐ Work with an attorney to establish a will for the orderly distribution of assets upon your death. If there is no will, state law determines how assets are distributed.

Depending on your need for Medicaid, your estate—in particular, your home—may be subject to the Medicaid Estate Recovery process. To protect your home from recovery, consider taking the steps in the checklist below. Realize, however, that some states have different recovery rules that may allow Medicaid to recover your home regardless of any legal documents allowing heirs to inherit the home.

Checklist: How to protect your home

Establishing a life estate:

- A life estate is a form of joint property ownership between two or more people.

- A life estate has two parties of interest: the life tenant and the remainder tenant.

- Life tenants (typically you and/or your spouse) have the right to live in the home for the remainder of their life. As such, they have the responsibility to pay mortgage payments, property taxes, home insurance, maintenance costs, etc., just as if they were the sole owner.

- Remainder tenants (typically a child or children of the life tenant) gain ownership of the property upon the life tenant's death. If there is more than one life tenant, then ownership transfers upon the death of the last remaining life tenant.

- With a life estate, the life tenant is not allowed to sell the property to others without the consent of the remainder tenants. If the life tenant sells the property on their own, they can only sell it for the duration of their life. Upon their death, the ownership of the property reverts to the remainder tenants even if the property was sold to a third party by the life tenant.

☐ Remainder tenants are not allowed to displace the life tenants from their home or sell the property without the life tenants' consent, because they have no legal right to the property while the life tenant is still living. Because they have no right to the property while the life tenant is alive, creditors have no claim on the property if the remainder tenants have financial or legal issues.

Credit: alexmisu

☐ Property in a life estate does not have to go through probate upon the life tenant's death, thus avoiding court fees and potentially recovery through the Medicaid Estate Recovery program, depending on the state's Medicaid recovery laws.

☐ If the property is placed in a life estate more than 5 years before the life tenant applies for Medicaid, the transfer of property cannot incur a Medicaid penalty when the life tenant applies to Medicaid for long-term care benefits. Therefore, if you may potentially need Medicaid in the future, it is best to establish the life estate as soon as possible so it falls outside the look-back period.

☐ If you need Medicaid in the near future, you should not establish a life estate because it will be counted as a gift during the Medicaid look-back period and you will have to wait through the penalty period before Medicaid begins to pay.

- [ ] If you need Medicaid and it has not been 5 years since the establishment of the life estate, the remainder tenants can voluntarily revert ownership back to the life tenant to avoid the Medicaid penalty. Remainder tenants are not required by law to revert ownership, so the life tenant should choose remainder tenants who will make choices that benefit the life tenant.

Establishing a trust:

- [ ] You may also protect your home from Medicaid Estate Recovery by transferring the home to an irrevocable trust.

- [ ] An irrevocable trust is a trust that cannot be changed by the grantor, or the person who created the trust. This means that once your home is placed in the trust, you cannot remove it from the trust without the written consent of the beneficiaries.

- [ ] To place a home in the trust, you will need to use a deed to transfer legal title of the property to the trust. After this, all insurance, property tax, and maintenance should be paid by the trust, so you may need to transfer cash to the trust to pay these bills if the trust does not have other available funds. Make sure that you notify the insurance company of the sale so the proper owner can be named in the insurance documents.

- [ ] If you still owe money on your mortgage, you will need to check the conditions of the mortgage before transferring the title to the trust. Some mortgage companies have a "due on transfer" clause that would require you to pay the remainder of the mortgage at the time the property is transferred to the trust.

☐ Putting a home in an irrevocable trust exempts it from estate taxes, but it may be subject to a gift tax. Discuss the tax implications of this move with a qualified tax advisor or estate planner.

☐ If you place your home in the irrevocable trust, you still have the right to live in the home until your death, but you should make sure this is stated in the terms of the trust.

☐ If you are living in a home that is owned and insured by a trust, you will need to consider purchasing renters' insurance to insure the contents of the home (your personal possessions).

☐ Unlike a revocable trust, the grantor is not allowed to be the trustee of an irrevocable trust (i.e., they cannot manage the trust). In addition, to prevent the assets of the trust from being counted as assets for Medicaid purposes, you and your spouse should not be listed as beneficiaries of the trust.

☐ Placing a home in an irrevocable trust protects it from claims against creditors. For example, if you need Medicaid coverage for long-term care services, Medicaid cannot place a lien on your home. In addition, Medicaid cannot claim the house after your death because the home is no longer part of your estate.

☐ Similar to the life estate, if you place your home in the irrevocable trust within 5 years of needing to apply for Medicaid, you will face a Medicaid penalty equal to the value of the house plus the value of the cash transferred to pay for insurance and property tax. Unlike the life estate, the irrevocable trust cannot be reversed to prevent the Medicaid penalty. Because the value of homes is generally high, the penalty period will be very long. It is better to wait until after the 5-year look-back period is past before applying for Medicaid.

☐ Because the value of the cash or other assets transferred to the trust for insurance and property tax can be counted against you for Medicaid benefits within the 5-year look-back period, you should transfer enough money to the trust to cover these expenses for many years. However, depending on the size of the house and level of insurance chosen, the Medicaid penalty for transferring money to the trust to cover these expenses should be fairly short if you transfer money annually.

☐ If you place your home in an irrevocable trust close to the time that it will need to be sold to pay back Medicaid, the formation of the trust may be considered fraudulent, and you may lose your home anyway. If you want to place your home in an irrevocable trust, it should be done as soon as possible.

Knowing how to protect your assets, including your home, is an important step in managing your finances and paying for healthcare. However, you will also need to understand the sources of income that may be available to you, including retirement benefits, Social Security, and veteran's benefits.

Retirement Benefits

During your working life, you will probably accrue money in a retirement account of some kind. Generally, these plans are established either in conjunction with an employer or as an individual retirement account.

Employers establish qualified plans to provide retirement benefits for their employees, and such plans can take the form of defined benefit plans or defined contribution plans. A defined benefit plan promises a specified monthly benefit at retirement. This monthly benefit lasts for the rest of the individual's life. The amount of the benefit is usually calculated based on the individual's salary and years of service. The two main types of defined benefit plans are pension plans and cash-balance plans.

In comparison, with a defined contribution plan, the employee or the employer (or both) contribute to the employee's individual account under the plan. Contributions are invested on the employee's behalf, and the employee ultimately receives the balance in their account at retirement. The value of these plans is not set but can increase or decrease depending on changes in the value of the underlying investments. The most common types of defined contribution plans include 401(k)s and 403(b)s.

Individual retirement accounts (IRAs) are opened with financial institutions. Several types of IRAs exist, including traditional IRAs and Roth IRAs, each with their own tax implications and rules regulating use. Although IRAs are not necessarily linked with an employer, they can be a valuable source of income for a person with chronic terminal illness.

You may work at several institutions over the course of your career, and it can be easy to lose track of retirement plans with former employers. If you have not already done so, it is a good idea to check with all of your former employers (and your spouse's former employers) for any forgotten retirement plans.

Credit: baki

Checklist: Basics about defined benefit plans

General:

☐ Defined benefit plans are typically funded by the employer, not the employee, and the employer retains the investment risk associated with the plan.

☐ The amount of the retirement payouts to employees is usually based on the employee's salary and years of service, but the formula used to calculate benefits differs with different types of plans.

☐ The two types of defined benefit plans are pension plans and cash-balance plans.

☐ The benefits in most defined benefit plans are protected by federal insurance through the Pension Benefit Guaranty Corporation (PBGC).

Pensions:

☐ Pension plans were designed to benefit employees who stayed with one employer for their entire career, with benefits increasing substantially the closer they get to retirement.

☐ Pensions promise a regular monthly benefit for the rest of the employee's life after they retire. The amount of this benefit is usually determined based on the employee's years of service, salary, and other factors, but it can also be simply a defined dollar amount.

☐ For most pension plans, the monthly benefit is based on the employee's average salary over their last five years of employment before retirement rather than on their average career salary, thus increasing retirement benefits as the employee's salary increases.

□ Pension plans were much more common several decades ago, so if you have worked at the same company for many years, you may have a pension plan through your employer.

□ Pensions are sometimes portable and insured, so it's possible that you have a forgotten pension from a company that no longer exists or that employed you many years ago. Tracking down lost pensions can be difficult but financially rewarding.

□ Pensions can be paid to a surviving spouse in some circumstances, so if you are a widow or widower, you may want to investigate your late spouse's retirement benefits to determine if you can access any remaining retirement funds.

Cash-balance plans:

□ Cash-balance plans function much like regular pension plans, but with a few elements borrowed from defined contribution plans.

□ In a cash-balance plan, your retirement benefits are based on a percentage of your salary plus calculated interest over the life of your employment. This amount is recorded in a hypothetical account. For example, the account balance increases by an amount equal to 6% of your salary each year, plus 5% interest on the previous year's account balance. The interest amount is usually based on the current

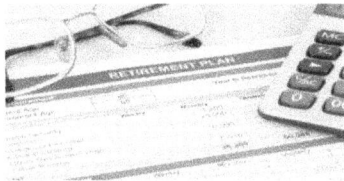

Credit: Casper1774 Studio

interest gained from investing in one-year Treasury bills.

- [ ] When you retire or leave the company, you are entitled to the balance of your hypothetical account. With these funds, you can either purchase an annuity equal to the balance of the account, or you can receive a lump sum equal to the balance of the account.

- [ ] If you purchase the annuity, you will receive monthly benefits for the rest of your life after retirement similar to a typical pension plan. The amount of the benefits will depend on the value of the annuity, the number of years until you begin to draw on the annuity, and whether the annuity has fixed or variable payments.

- [ ] If you elect to receive a lump sum, this money can usually be rolled over into an IRA or other retirement fund.

Checklist: Basics about defined contribution plans

General:

- [ ] For most defined contribution plans, the employee decides how much they want to contribute to their retirement account. These funds are deducted directly from their paycheck and transferred to their retirement account. Thus, the employee is the main contributor to defined contribution plans.

- [ ] Most companies also contribute to the employee's retirement account based on company limits, the employee's contribution amounts, and the employee's salary. Many companies will match the employee's contribution up to a certain percentage of the employee's salary.

- Employers typically use a technique called "vesting" so that their matched funds are not available until an employee has worked for the company for a specified number of years (usually three or four).

- Typically, the employer hires an investment firm to invest the contributions and manage the accounts. The investment firm then provides participating employees with the option of investing in one or more mutual funds based on investment strategy.

- The risks and rewards associated with the plan investments rest completely on the employee rather than the employer, but the employee also has more control over their investment decisions.

401(k) plans:

- The annual limit for 401(k) contributions in 2020 is $19,500 for those under age 50 and $26,000 for those age 50 and older.

- Funds in a 401(k) account, including earnings after deposit, are taxed when they are withdrawn during retirement, not when they are deposited.

- If an employee withdraws money from their 401(k) before the age of 59 ½, the withdrawal may be assessed a 10% penalty, plus regular taxation. However, this penalty can be waived if the money is used to treat a sudden disability or prevent home foreclosure.

- After the employee turns 70 ½, they must make required minimum withdrawals from the account.

- Certain 401(k) plans also offer shares of the employer's stock.

Roth 401(k) plans:

- Roth 401(k) plans are similar to traditional 401(k) plans, except that funds are taxed at the time of contribution rather than the time of withdrawal.

- Roth 401(k) accounts are beneficial for individuals who believe they will be in a higher tax bracket after retirement than when the funds are contributed and for those who have many years to let their contributions grow. Because of this, Roth 401(k) accounts are usually most beneficial to younger individuals.

- Roth 401(k) plans are relatively new (began in 2006), so you may not have a retirement plan of this type.

- Individuals can contribute to a Roth 401(k) up to the same limit as the traditional 401(k), but the sum total deposited in 401(k) and Roth 401(k) accounts cannot be greater than the limit. For example, an individual under the age of 50 could deposit $19,500 in a traditional 401(k) account OR in a Roth 401(k) account, but not both. However, if desired, they could split the $19,500 between the two types of retirement accounts.

- In contrast to Roth IRA accounts, anyone, regardless of their income, can contribute to a Roth 401(k) account if it is offered by their employer.

- If an employee chooses to contribute to a Roth 401(k) account, any employer matching funds will still be deposited in a traditional 401(k) account.

- Once money is deposited in a Roth 401(k) account, it can never be reverted to a traditional 401(k) account.

- ☐ If you wait until you are 59 ½ to make withdrawals from your Roth 401(k) plan, and if you have participated in the plan for a minimum of 5 years, all funds withdrawn from the account are tax-free, including earnings.

- ☐ If desired, employees can roll over their Roth 401(k) account to a Roth IRA account when their employment terminates.

- ☐ If the plan permits, you may be able to take a loan from your Roth 401(k) account. The maximum amount of the loan and the repayment plan are usually specified in the plan's rules and guidelines.

403(b) plans:

- ☐ These plans are nearly identical to 401(k) plans, except they are only offered to certain employees of public schools, colleges, and universities; tax-exempt organizations such as charities and some hospitals; and some ministers.

- ☐ Contributions to a 403(b) account can be placed in an annuity through an insurance company, a custodial account invested in mutual funds, or a retirement income account for church employees. These choices are usually more limited than with a 401(k) plan.

- ☐ Employer matching funds may be vested more quickly in 403(b) plans than in similar 401(k) plans.

- ☐ You may be able to withdraw money from your 403(b) account without penalty before age 59 ½ if you have a financial hardship. Each plan has a different definition of financial hardship, so check with your plan to determine if any penalties would apply for early withdrawal.

- These plans are also sometimes offered in a Roth form, where funds are taxed at the time of contribution rather than the time of withdrawal.

457(b) plans:

- These plans are also similar to 401(k) plans, except they are only available to state and local government employees, as well as employees of certain tax-exempt organizations.

- If an employer offers both a 457(b) plan and a 401(k) plan, employees can invest in both, and therefore potentially double their retirement contribution for the year.

- In the three years prior to retirement, individuals can contribute either twice the normal limit or an amount equal to the underutilized limit in previous years, whichever is less, as a special catch-up contribution if the plan allows it.

- There are no penalties for making early withdrawals from a 457(b) plan. However, all withdrawals, regardless of age, are still subject to regular income taxation.

- A Roth form is available for 457(b) plans. Similar to other Roth plans, funds are taxed at the time of contribution rather than at withdrawal.

Thrift savings plans:

- These plans are similar to 401(k) plans, except they are only available to employees of the U.S. government, including the armed services.

- The thrift savings plan allows employees to invest in six different funds: government security fund, fixed-income fund, common stock fund, small cap stock fund, international stock fund, and life cycle fund.

☐ Money can be transferred to a thrift savings plan from another retirement account upon enrollment in the Federal service, and money can be transferred from the thrift savings plan to another retirement account when you leave the Federal service.

☐ Individuals who make tax-exempt contributions to their thrift savings plan while deployed in a designated combat zone cannot exceed the annual addition limit, up to $57,000 in 2020.

☐ As of 2012, thrift savings plans began offering a Roth option, in which contributions are taxed rather than withdrawals. This allows earnings to grow tax free.

☐ Individuals who are deployed in a tax-exempt designated combat zone are allowed to contribute tax-exempt earnings to the Roth thrift savings plan, allowing them to never pay taxes on those contributions. However, the Roth funds are limited to the normal $19,500 per year contribution for individuals under the age of 50.

Employee stock ownership plans (ESOPs):

☐ In an ESOP, the company sets up a trust fund with either cash or shares of company stock, and each employee receives shares of stock as compensation.

☐ The shares are held in the trust fund and distributed to employees when they retire or leave the company. At that time, the employee can either sell the shares on the open market (for public companies) or sell them back to the company for cash (for public or private companies).

☐ Employees must work for the company for a specific number of years to be "vested" in the plan before they are eligible to receive their shares of stock.

Profit-sharing and stock bonus plans:

☐ In a profit-sharing plan, the company contributes money from their profits to a trust. The trustee then manages the investments in the trust, and employees are listed as beneficiaries of the trust.

☐ Companies must allow all employees to participate in the profit-sharing plan. They cannot favor managers and higher-level employees and exclude lower-level employees.

☐ Contributions to the profit-sharing plan are entirely from the employer and not the employee. The employer can determine each year what portion of the company's profits will be contributed to the plan. However, employers are not required to make a contribution.

☐ Profit-sharing plans use a formula that allocates a portion of each annual contribution to each employee. Employers are allowed to contribute up to 100% of each employee's compensation or up to $57,000, whichever is less.

☐ Stock bonus plans are similar to profit-sharing plans except employees have the right to demand their distribution be in shares of company stock rather than in cash.

☐ Profit-sharing and stock bonus plans may also incorporate a 401(k) plan.

Money purchase plans:

- ☐ Money purchase plans are similar to profit-sharing plans, except the employer is required to contribute to the plan each year.

- ☐ The employer is required to contribute an amount equal to a certain percentage of the employee's salary—5%, for example—every year.

- ☐ Unlike profit-sharing plans, both employers and employees are allowed to contribute to a money purchase plan.

- ☐ Contributions are invested for the employee, and each employee's retirement benefit is based on the value of the contributions to their account and the gains or losses the account has experienced.

Checklist: Individual retirement arrangements (IRAs)

General:

- ☐ IRAs are retirement accounts that individuals, self-employed persons, and small businesses open with banks.

- ☐ There are four main types of IRAs: traditional IRAs, Roth IRAs, SEP IRAs, and SIMPLE IRAs.

- ☐ IRAs can hold a variety of investments, including stocks, bonds, and mutual funds.

- ☐ Contribution limits for traditional and Roth IRAs combined are $6,000 for individuals under age 50 and $7,000 for individuals age 50 and over.

- ☐ Individuals can contribute to IRAs even if they contribute to a retirement account at their place of employment.

- [ ] IRAs cannot be jointly owned, but the amount left in the IRA after the owner's death can be paid to a beneficiary.

Traditional IRAs:

- [ ] Similar to 401(k) plans, individuals are taxed on distributions or withdrawals from a traditional IRA rather than their contributions. Therefore, earnings on the contributions are also taxed at the time of withdrawal. Distributions must be included in the individual's income tax return for the year of withdrawal.

- [ ] Although contributions to an IRA may be tax-deductible, individuals with higher income who are also covered by a retirement plan at work may not be able to take a full deduction.

- [ ] Individuals can contribute to a traditional IRA if they earn taxable income and are under age 70 ½. Individuals over age 70 ½ cannot contribute to a traditional IRA.

- [ ] Individuals who are under the age of 59 ½ and want to withdraw funds from their traditional IRA will be charged an early withdrawal fee of 10%. However, this penalty may be waived if the distribution is needed to pay unreimbursed medical expenses, if the owner of the account has a disability, or for other qualifying reasons.

- [ ] Individuals who are between the age of 59 ½ and 70 ½ can withdraw funds from their traditional IRA with no penalty, and they can withdraw any amount.

- [ ] Individuals who are age 70 ½ or older must begin withdrawing required minimum annual distributions. The minimum distribution can be calculated using a worksheet supplied by the IRS. This amount may change every year, so make sure this calculation is done correctly. Individuals may withdraw any amount, as long as it is over the required minimum distribution. If the amount is less than the required minimum distribution, you will pay a 50% excise tax on the portion of the money that was not distributed as required.

Roth IRAs:

☐ Roth IRAs are similar to traditional IRAs except that contributions to these accounts are taxed, whereas withdrawals are not. Earnings are allowed to grow tax-free.

☐ Individuals with higher incomes are not allowed to contribute the maximum to a Roth IRA and may not be able to contribute anything at all. In 2020, single individuals with income higher than $124,000 and married individuals filing jointly with income higher than $196,000 cannot contribute the maximum to a Roth IRA. Single individuals with income higher than $139,000 and married individuals filing jointly with income higher than $206,000 cannot contribute directly to a Roth IRA.

☐ As long as income requirements are met, any adult can contribute to a Roth IRA at any time, regardless of age. Even individuals older than 70 ½ can continue to contribute to a Roth IRA.

☐ Many types of retirement plans can be rolled over into a Roth IRA account, but the amount rolled over will be taxable if it came from a non-Roth account. For example, money rolled over from a 401(k) account would be taxed upon rollover, but money from a Roth 401(k) account would not be taxed.

☐ Individuals who are under the age of 59 ½ and want to withdraw funds from their Roth IRA can withdraw their original contributions with no penalty if the account has been open for at least 5 years. If they withdraw earnings before the age of 59 ½, they will be subject to a 10% early withdrawal fee, and the earnings will be taxed.

☐ Individuals who are over the age of 59 ½ can withdraw any amount at any time with no penalty, as long as the account has been open for at least 5 years. Both original contributions and earnings can be withdrawn tax-free.

☐ In contrast to traditional IRAs, individuals are not required to take minimum distributions from a Roth IRA when they reach age 70 ½. The money can remain in the account untouched to be passed on to the next generation if desired.

SEP IRAs:

☐ SEP IRAs are most commonly used by small business owners or self-employed individuals. However, a business of any size can open a SEP IRA as long as they do not offer any other type of retirement account.

☐ SEP IRAs are usually combined with the individual's traditional IRA as one account. The SEP IRA portion of the account is for contributions made by the employer, and the traditional IRA portion of the account is for contributions made by the employee. Employees are not allowed to contribute to SEP IRAs.

□ The employer can contribute an amount up to 25% of the company's net earnings or $57,000, whichever is less. Employers

can decide how much they want to contribute within this limit, and the contribution amount may change for each period depending on the financial state of the company. Catch-up contributions are not allowed in SEP IRAs.

□ The limits for contribution to a SEP IRA account and a traditional IRA account do not affect each other. Both the employer and the employee can maximize their contributions based on federal laws. However, participation in an employer-funded SEP IRA may reduce the tax deduction that the employee can take for their traditional IRA contributions.

□ As with a traditional IRA, funds are taxed at the time of withdrawal. Employees do not pay taxes at the time of contribution.

□ Distribution rules and penalties are the same as for traditional IRAs.

SIMPLE IRAs:

□ Savings Incentive Match Plan for Employees (SIMPLE) IRAs are intended for small business (fewer than 100 employees) and self-employed individuals. The employer cannot offer any other retirement plan if they provide a SIMPLE IRA.

☐ As with a traditional IRA, funds are taxed at the time of withdrawal rather than at the time of contribution.

☐ These accounts are much like SEP IRAs, except that employees can make contributions. Employees are allowed to contribute up to $13,500 to their SIMPLE IRA account in 2020. Individuals age 50 or over can make catch-up contributions up to $3,000 in 2020.

☐ In SIMPLE IRAs, employers are required to contribute to their employees' SIMPLE IRAs using either matching or nonelective contributions.

☐ With matching contributions, employers contribute a dollar-for-dollar matching contribution up to 3% of the employee's salary. Employees that do not contribute do not receive matching funds that year. The percentage the employer matches can be lower than 3% in two out of every five years.

☐ With nonelective contributions, the employer contributes a flat 2% of the employee's compensation, regardless employee contribution.

☐ Participation in a SIMPLE IRA does not prevent you from participating in a traditional or Roth IRA.

☐ Distribution rules and penalties are the same as for traditional IRAs, except if you withdraw money within the first two years of the account opening and you are under the age of 59 ½, you will be charged a 25% penalty.

Once you have determined which types of retirement accounts you have and what withdrawal stipulations each account follows, you can collect benefits from the retirement accounts to help pay your bills, both medical and non-medical. The checklist below describes the information you must have to begin collecting retirement income.

Checklist: Information needed to receive retirement benefits

- ☐ Name

- ☐ Contact information

- ☐ Date of birth, with birth certificate

- ☐ Spouse's date of birth, with birth certificate

- ☐ Marital status, with marriage certificate

- ☐ Social Security number

- ☐ Type of benefit being sought

- ☐ Retirement account information

- ☐ Retirement date

If you have multiple types of retirement accounts, consider talking to a qualified financial advisor or accountant to make sure you are meeting all the requirements for minimum distributions. If you are under the age of 59 ½ and you need to take distributions from your retirement accounts to cover expenses, a financial advisor or accountant can also walk you through the fees and penalties that may be associated with that withdrawal and help you determine if you qualify for withdrawal without penalty.

Chapter 4:
Out of Pocket Alternatives

If you do not have retirement benefits, are concerned that your benefits will not be sufficient to meet your needs, or you are under age 59 ½ and do not want to make an early withdrawal from your benefits, you may want to explore other options for preserving and stretching your personal wealth. Two trends for saving money on healthcare are on the rise—medical tourism and Canadian pharmaceuticals. These trends have been making news for several years now, and each has potential benefits and consequences.

Medical Tourism

The term medical tourism is used to describe people who travel from one location to another to receive medical, dental, or surgical treatments. While some medical tourists travel domestically for care—from one city or state to another—the term is typically applied to people who travel internationally for treatment.

The main reason people become medical tourists is affordability. Cost-savings estimates for popular medical tourism destinations range from 35%-60% off typical U.S. prices. A main contributor to these savings is the fact that hospitals in other countries pay physicians and healthcare workers less than hospitals in the United States and have lower overhead expenses than their U.S. counterparts. In addition, malpractice insurance costs in other countries tend to be lower than in the United States. In many cases, the total cost of care received abroad plus travel expenses for the patient and their spouse is less than or equal to the cost of care alone in the United States.

Another reason people become medical tourists is better access to care. Depending on the area of the United States in which an individual lives and the type of specialty care they are seeking, travel—whether domestic or international—may be necessary to receive care in a timely fashion. Certain procedures may also be available in other countries that are no longer available or are not yet available in the United States.

Common services sought by medical tourists include cosmetic procedures, fertility procedures, cardiology procedures, and orthopedic procedures. General surgeries—including laparoscopic options—and oncology services are widely available as well. Medical tourists from the United States usually seek treatment in South and Central America and the Caribbean; Thailand and India are also common destinations. Mexico is a popular destination for dental care. Often, healthcare providers in popular medical tourism destinations have received at least a portion of their training in the United States. In addition, several large U.S. medical schools have engaged in joint initiatives with foreign hospitals, including Harvard, Johns Hopkins, and Duke University.

Many countries and cities outside of the United States actively solicit medical tourists, including Dubai, Singapore, and Malaysia. In addition, healthcare brokers in the United States and abroad help arrange air travel, hotel accommodations, hospital admission, and physician access for medical tourists.

Medical tourists typically pay for care at the time of service, and many insurers do not pay for care in foreign countries unless it is rendered in emergency situations. However, some providers and large employers form alliances with hospitals in other countries in efforts to control healthcare costs. Anyone considering medical tourism should check their insurance policy before planning a procedure in another country.

Medical tourism has been associated with complications, and procedure type and destination are primary factors in determining risk. One of the biggest concerns for medical tourists is infection by antibiotic-resistant strains of bacteria. Antibiotic resistance is a global problem, and resistant bacteria are more common outside of the United States. For example, patients who recently had cosmetic surgery in the Dominican Republic contracted nontuberculous mycobacteria infections. Medication quality is another risk associated with medical tourism in some countries. Medications may be counterfeit, of poor quality, or past their expiration date.

Additional risks are associated with air travel following surgery and during recovery periods. Flying and surgery both increase the risk of developing blood clots and pulmonary emboli. This is especially true for individuals who have had chest or abdominal surgery. Engaging in sight-seeing and other vacation-related activities following a procedure abroad also has the potential to produce complications in the postoperative period.

When weighing the risks and benefits of medical tourism, always check the credentials of the facility where the procedure will take place and the qualifications of the healthcare provider performing the procedure. In doing so, be aware that local standards for care facilities and providers may be different from those in the United States. Some accrediting groups—including the Joint Commission, DNV International Accreditation for Hospitals, and the International Society for Quality in Health Care—provide international accreditation for care facilities. The American College of Surgeons (ACS) also recommends seeking care from physicians or providers certified in their specialties through a process equivalent to that used by the American Board of Medical Specialties. The American Medical Association has developed similar recommendations. The ACS, American Society of Plastic Surgeons, and the International Society of Aesthetic Plastic Surgery all offer international surgical accreditation. If relying on a private company or healthcare broker to arrange your care, ask about the accreditation requirements they use to identify facilities and providers. Remember, however, that using an accredited facility or provider does not guarantee a complication-free procedure, as is true with any provider or facility in the United States.

The following checklists include some additional things you can do to help prepare for a procedure as a medical tourist and things you can do to promote a healthy recovery before and after returning home.

Checklist: Preparing for medical tourism

☐ Be sure that any current medical conditions are well controlled and make sure that your regular healthcare provider knows about your travel and medical care plans.

☐ If traveling internationally for care, visit a travel medicine specialist 4–6 weeks prior to your departure. Discuss general information for healthy travel and specific risks related to the planned procedure. Also be sure to discuss any anticipated restrictions to travel following the procedure.

☐ Secure all necessary travel documents. This includes a passport and may include a visa, depending upon your destination. U.S. passports cost about $150. It typically takes six to eight weeks to receive a passport, though the application process can be expedited for an additional fee. If you already have a passport, ensure that it will be valid for at least six months after your return home. Prior to scheduling your trip, contact the embassy of the country to which you will be traveling to find out if a visa is required for your visit. Application process, cost, and time frame for visa issuance varies with country, so be sure to check the requirements well in advance of travel.

☐ Receive any needed vaccinations and medications related to your travel destination. Fill any regular maintenance prescriptions.

☐ Secure a written agreement with the healthcare facility or the group arranging your trip. The agreement should define what treatments you will receive, what supplies will be provided, and the specific care items covered in the upfront costs.

☐ If traveling to a country where you do not speak the language, develop a plan for dealing with potential communication problems ahead of time. Determine how you will communicate with your doctor and other care providers.

☐ Obtain copies of your medical records to take along on the trip. Records should include lab work or other studies that relate to the care you are planning to receive. They should also outline any allergies you have.

☐ Prepare a list of all prescriptions and over-the-counter medications that you take. Be sure to include brand names, generic names, manufacturers, and dosages.

☐ Schedule an appointment with your regular physician for post-procedure follow-up care prior to leaving for your trip.

Checklist: Promoting healthy recovery

☐ Obtain copies of all medical records related to your procedure before being discharged from the medical facility.

☐ Save any outer packaging and package inserts from medications you were given or that you purchased while abroad.

☐ If staying in a hotel following discharge and prior to returning home, notify hotel staff that you have undergone a medical procedure and will be recovering. Make any necessary arrangements for food, laundry, and additional care.

☐ If you choose to do typical tourist activities following your procedure, do not engage in activities incompatible with your recovery, such as consuming alcohol or swimming. Take care to avoid overexertion and overexposure to the sun.

☐ Wait an appropriate amount of time to return home. Typically, you should avoid air travel for at least 10 days following chest or abdominal surgery and 7–10 days following laser or cosmetic procedures to the face, eyelids, or nose.

☐ If possible, make necessary airport arrangements several days in advance. Schedule wheelchair transportation through the terminal if you feel it is necessary. Secure documentation from your doctor indicating that you've recently undergone a procedure and may require specialized security screening. Notify the airline of your condition and request extra time to board the plane.

☐ Upon returning home, visit your regular physician for follow-up care.

☐ Watch for signs of infection and other complications. These may include but are not limited to fever, swelling, redness, wound drainage, and pain. If you notice these signs or experience any other symptoms you believe are related to your procedure, seek medical care immediately.

When seeking care for possible complications of an international surgery, be sure to take along any medical records and medication information provided by the facility where the procedure was performed. Do not delay seeking treatment. Medical tourists sometimes fear embarrassment or other negative repercussions when seeking care following their return home. As a result, they may ignore signs that something is wrong or delay seeking care in the hope that the problem will clear up on its own. This can worsen complications and have serious negative consequences to health. While your regular doctor is within their rights to decline to provide follow-up care for any procedure (no matter where it was performed), they have an ethical responsibility to refer you to another physician who is capable of providing the services you need.

Canadian Pharmaceuticals

Due to the high costs of prescription drugs in the United States, many consumers turn to Canadian pharmacies to fill prescriptions that they otherwise could not afford. Some of these individuals are uninsured, some are insured but their prescriptions are not covered, and some have found that Canadian prescription prices are cheaper than the insurance out-of-pocket payments for their medications.

Canadian pharmaceuticals have long had a reputation for being cheaper than similar drugs sold in the United States. For example, the cholesterol drug Lipitor typically costs $150 in the United States, while the same dose sells for $50 in Canada. The primary reason for this difference is that the Canadian government sets the prices for all patented drugs while the United States allows the market to set its own price.

In Canada, drug companies submit price proposals and sales information to the Patented Medicine Prices Review Board (PMPRB). The board compares the proposals to the costs of similar therapies in other industrialized nations to establish a price ceiling. If the company's quote comes in under the price ceiling, the company can sell the drug at that price. If it comes in above the price ceiling, the drug company and PMPRB negotiate a price. In the event that the PMPRB and the drug company cannot reach an agreement, the Federal court makes a ruling about the price. The Canadian government will not approve a drug for the Canadian market if a manufacturer refuses to sell it for the set price.

In the United States, costs for drugs are essentially set by what the market will bear. There is not a governmental body—as there is in Canada—that sets the price. In addition, the amount that consumers pay varies widely based on whether they are insured, which insurance company they use, and what type of insurance plan they have.

It is illegal for U.S. citizens to purchase drugs outside of the United States and import them into the country. The rule exists because the Food and Drug Administration (FDA) has no way to regulate the quality and safety of drugs sold in other countries. The FDA acknowledges that the drug standards of other highly developed nations—including Canada—are comparable to those of the United States. In some cases, the drugs sold in these countries are produced in the United States. Drugs may be produced in other countries as well, and this is where

Credit: Shutterstock

the problem lies—the FDA has no means of ensuring that cheap imports produced in China and other less-developed nations are not making their way into markets outside of the United States. Drugs such as these may be counterfeit, misbranded, or expired. They are also prone to quality issues, like containing too large a dose of medication, too small a dose of medication, or impure or harmful filler ingredients. Biologics and other medications that require refrigeration are of special concern due to the high likelihood of improper handling at during the transportation process.

Problematic copycat drugs are generally not a concern with drugs purchased through reputable brick-and-mortar pharmacies in Canada. Such pharmacies are regulated in much the same way as similar U.S. pharmacies and require that prescriptions be written by Canadian physicians. However, copycats are a legitimate problem with online Canadian prescription sellers that cater to U.S. consumers. In some cases, these online storefronts are not actually pharmacies; rather, they are clearinghouses that gather consumers' orders and pass them on to dispensing pharmacies. While these pharmacies are, in theory, licensed and regulated, it is difficult for the Canadian authorities to police them and determine from what country the drugs they distribute were sourced.

In spite of its illegality and the risk of purchasing sub-quality medications, price is a primary reason why many Americans continue to rely on Canadian drugs. Another reason is the fact that enforcement of the FDA's no importation rule is generally lax. Enforcement is complicated because medications can cross into the country by post or be carried in at border crossings and other ports of entry. In addition, the FDA rule is enforced by other federal agencies—U.S. Customs and Border Protection (CBP) and the Transportation Security Administration (TSA). The restrictions related to prescriptions vary from agency to agency and from product to product, and individuals who are traveling across the border are allowed to carry medications for personal use during their travels. The following checklists outline the FDA's, CBP's, and TSA's regulations for carrying personal medications in this situation.

Checklist: FDA guidelines for traveling with personal medication

☐ Carry a valid prescription or doctor's note with you. The note must be written in English.

☐ Keep the medication in its original container with the doctor's instructions printed on the bottle. If you no longer have the original container, carry a copy of your prescription or a letter from your doctor explaining why you need the medication.

☐ Travel with only as much medication as you need for your personal use. This should be no more than a 90-day supply.

☐ Transport only FDA-approved medications. The FDA does not allow passage of unapproved versions of drugs from foreign countries. This often includes generic medications produced outside of the United States.

Checklist: CBP guidelines for traveling with personal medication

☐ Carry only the amount of medicine you will need during your travel. This means no more than a 90-day supply for most medications and no more than 50 dosage units of controlled substances.

☐ Declare all drugs and medicinals to a CBP official.

- ☐ Carry medications in their original containers.

- ☐ Carry a prescription or written statement from your doctor stating that the substances are being used under a doctor's supervision and are necessary to maintain your health.

- ☐ For prescribed controlled substances, ensure that the prescription is issued by a practitioner licensed in the United States who is registered with and authorized by the Drug Enforcement Administration (DEA).

- ☐ Transport only medications that can be legally prescribed in the United States.

Checklist: TSA guidelines for traveling with personal medication

- ☐ Present liquid medication to a TSA official. Other forms of medication, including pill and solid forms, do not need to be presented but will need to be screened.

- ☐ Medication can be placed in either carry-on or checked baggage, though carry-ons are recommended in case you need immediate access.

- ☐ Medications do not have to be carried in original containers per TSA guidelines, but individual state laws may require that they be.

- ☐ Unlimited amounts of pill and solid medications can be transported provided that they are screened.

- ☐ Medication screening is typically done via X-ray. If you do not want medications to be X-rayed, you may request a hand inspection instead.

An estimated 20 million Americans purchase their prescriptions from other countries, in spite of it being illegal to do so. Several times in the last two decades, lawmakers have sought to pass legislation that would make it legal to purchase prescription drugs from Canada. In addition, several states are currently pursuing legislation that would allow for importation of Canadian drugs. These lawmakers must contend not only with the FDA's safety concerns, but with pharmaceutical company lobbyists worried about the impact of Canadian imports on U.S. drug prices and sales.

Additional Titles from Omega Press

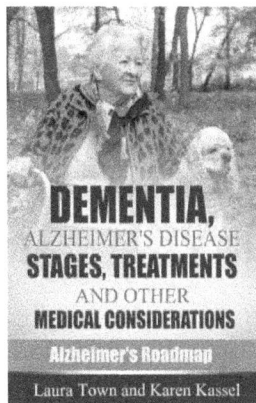

Know What to Expect

Dementia, Alzheimer's Disease Stages, Treatments, and Other Medical Considerations provides answers to the following questions and more:

- **What is Alzheimer's disease?** Learn what Alzheimer's disease is, including its characteristics, signs, and risk factors.
- **What can my loved one with Alzheimer's disease expect?** Read detailed descriptions of the stages of Alzheimer's disease, including what patients and caregivers can expect to see at each stage as the disease progresses.
- **What treatments are available?** A survey of prescription medications introduces you to the treatments available to help patients cope with the progression of the disease.
- **What about clinical trials?** Clinical trials are important to finding a cure for Alzheimer's disease, but this book describes the precautions for your loved one to consider before choosing to participate in them.
- **Is there audio for this book?** Yes, you can find the audiobook here: https://adbl.co/2SwzzlA

Chapter 5:
Government Assistance

If you were employed in a Social Security-eligible job or if you have low income, you may be eligible for government assistance to help pay for medical and non-medical expenses. Government programs that provide assistance include Social Security and SNAP (Supplemental Nutrition Assistance Program).

Social Security

If you have a terminal illness and were employed (and therefore paid Social Security taxes), you likely qualify for income benefits from the Social Security Administration (SSA),

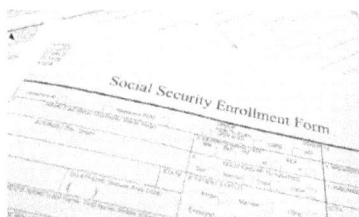

Credit: zimmytws

even if you are not yet full retirement age. Social Security (SS) benefits come in three forms: retirement benefits, disability benefits, and supplemental security income (SSI).

Checklist: Basics about Social Security retirement benefits

☐ During the years you worked and paid SS taxes, you earned "credits" toward SS benefits. To qualify for SS retirement benefits, you need 40 credits. One credit is received each quarter that SS taxes are paid, which equals 10 years of work before you qualify for SS benefits.

☐ Your benefit payment is based on how much you earned during your working career. Higher lifetime earnings result in higher benefits. You can estimate your benefit online using the Retirement Estimator.

☐ You can get SS retirement benefits as early as 62. However, you will receive a reduced benefit if you retire before you reach the full retirement age. You can delay your retirement payments up to age 70 if desired.

☐ If you were born in 1954 or earlier, you are already eligible for a full SS benefit. If you were born between 1955 and 1959, the age at which full retirement benefits are payable increases gradually to age 67. Individuals born during or after 1960 are eligible for full benefits at the age of 67.

☐ If you are able to continue working past your full retirement age, you will increase your SS benefit upon retirement both because you had higher lifetime earnings and because SS increases your benefit by a certain percentage each year you don't claim retirement benefits.

☐ Widows and widowers can begin receiving SS benefits at age 60, or at age 50 if they have a disability and the disability started before or within 7 years of their spouse's death. If desired, the widow or widower can take reduced benefits on their late spouse's account until they reach full retirement age and then switch their benefits to their own account to start receiving full benefits.

☐ If you are eligible to receive full retirement benefits, sometimes your other family members, specifically your spouse and minor or disabled children, can also receive benefits, including spouses who are age 62 or older; former spouses who are 62 or older;

spouses who are younger than 62, if they are taking care of a child entitled on the retiree's record who is younger than age 16 or has a disability; children up to age 18 (or 19 if they have not yet graduated from high school); and children of any age with a disability.

☐ Some individuals who receive SS retirement benefits have to pay taxes on those benefits. Talk to a trusted tax advisor or accountant to determine if you will need to pay taxes.

☐ You can apply for retirement benefits online, or you can call the agency at 1-800-772-1213. You can also apply in person at any SS office. Certain information is required for enrollment, including the applicant's SS number, birth certificate, W-2 forms, and other documents.

If you have to retire early because of a terminal illness and you are not yet eligible to receive SS retirement benefits, you should consider applying for SS disability benefits. The amount of the disability benefit is the same as a full, unreduced retirement benefit. The process can take several months and may not be retroactive, so there may be months when you are disabled but do not receive disability income. Therefore, it is best to apply as early as possible once you meet the disability requirements.

Checklist: Basics about Social Security disability benefits

☐ Disability benefits are for individuals under age 65 who have been employed for a specified time, now have a disability, and are not currently receiving SS benefits. SS only pays for total disability, not partial disability.

- [ ] To meet the employment requirements, you must have accumulated enough credits to be eligible for Social Security benefits. Individuals aged 31 to 42 must have accumulated 20 credits. For every year after that, the amount increases by one credit until 40 credits are accumulated, which is the maximum number of credits needed. A maximum of 4 credits can be earned each year based on earnings.

- [ ] You must also meet Social Security's very strict definition of disability. You are considered disabled under SS rules if (1) you cannot do work you did before; (2) you cannot adjust to other work because of your medical condition(s); and (3) your disability has lasted or is expected to last for at least one year or to result in death.

- [ ] To help meet the disability requirements, you must provide proof of your diagnosis of and treatment for a debilitating terminal illness.

- [ ] Before you apply for SS disability, you should print and review the Adult Disability Checklist online. This checklist details documents that will be needed to apply for and receive disability benefits.

- [ ] Even if you do not have all the necessary documents listed in the checklist, don't delay in applying for disability benefits. SS will help you get whatever documents you need.

- [ ] To begin the disability application, fill out the Disability Benefit Application and the Medical Release Form online. You can also apply by phone at 1-800-772-1213 or in person by making an appointment at your local SS office.

- [ ] After you apply for disability, SS will provide confirmation of the application; review the application; contact you if the agency needs more information; inform you if other family members may be able to receive benefits on the applicant's record or if the applicant may be able to receive benefits on another person's record (such as a spouse or loved one); process the application; and mail their decision. This process usually takes a minimum of three to five months.

☐ Payments usually begin within a few months of the disability. The SSA requires a five-month waiting period before disability benefits can begin, so the first SS benefit will be paid for the sixth full month after the disability began. Payments are issued in the month after they are due. For example, you will receive your January disability check in February.

☐ You may also be eligible for back payments. Back payments allow you to be paid benefits for the months you were waiting for your application to be processed, assuming you are approved for disability benefits. The SSA will not pay for the first five months, but if your application took longer than five months to process, you may be eligible for back payments during the remaining months of the application process.

☐ If you have had a disability for many months before you submit the disability application, you may also be eligible for retroactive payments. If you can establish that the onset date of your disability was prior to your application date, the SSA may pay you for as many as 17 months

Credit: Andrey_Popov

(one year plus the 5-month waiting period) of disability benefits up to your onset date once your application is approved.

□ Like SS retirement benefits, the monthly disability benefit is based on your lifetime earnings. Therefore, the disability benefit will be different for each person. In addition, you may have to pay taxes on the benefits you receive similar to SS retirement benefits.

□ The SSA requires electronic transfer of funds, so you will want to set up electronic payments into a bank account.

□ If you should reach a point where you are unable to handle your own money, the SSA can send the benefit payments to another responsible individual who promises to use the funds to care for you. A caregiver or durable power of attorney is a good choice for receiving these funds on your behalf, but they must be approved by the SSA. This individual is called a representative payee. The representative payee is responsible for tracking how the money is spent or saved so they can prove that they are using the money to care for the intended individual. Financial reports will need to be filed annually by the representative payee.

□ In general, benefits will continue as long as you are disabled. However, the law requires that the SSA review the case periodically to see whether the person is still disabled. If your condition is unlikely to improve, these reviews will likely take place once every five to seven years.

□ Once you reach full retirement age, you will automatically begin receiving retirement benefits rather than disability benefits. The amount you receive each month should remain the same.

☐ Once you receive SS disability benefits for two years, you will automatically be enrolled in Medicare. You may also be eligible for the Supplemental Nutrition Assistance Program or for Medicaid.

In addition to retirement and disability benefits, SS also has a Supplemental Security Income (SSI) program for individuals who are blind, disabled, or over the age of 65 who meet specific income and asset requirements. The requirements for this program are similar to those for Medicaid assistance, and they are detailed in the following checklist.

Checklist: Basics about Supplemental Security Income (SSI)

☐ To determine if you are eligible for SSI benefits, you can use the Benefit Eligibility Screening Tool online.

☐ Income requirements are based off of monthly Federal benefit rates. Currently, these rates are $783 for an individual or $1,175 for a couple if they live on their own. Rates are decreased if they live with someone else and do not share housing costs. Countable income is then subtracted from this benefit rate to determine their SSI benefit. For example, a single individual living alone with $300 in countable income would receive an SSI benefit of $483 monthly.

☐ Asset or resource limits are $2,000 in countable assets for a single individual and $3,000 in countable assets for a couple. Assets include cash, bank accounts, stocks and bonds, land, vehicles, personal property, life insurance, and other resources that could be converted to cash. However, not all assets are countable assets. For example, your primary home, household goods and personal items, one vehicle, some burial funds, some life insurance policies, and SS benefits are not included as countable assets.

- [ ] If you qualify for SSI based on a disability, disability requirements are the same as for the SS disability benefits. In this case, you would be qualified to receive both SS disability and SSI benefits.

- [ ] Similarly, if you are at full retirement age, you are likely eligible for SS retirement benefits. Receiving SS disability or retirement benefits does not exempt you from receiving SSI benefits.

- [ ] You can apply for benefits online or schedule an appointment with the local SS office. To make an appointment, call 1-800-772-1213 from 7 a.m. to 7 p.m., Monday through Friday, or contact your local SS office directly. If you apply online, a Social Security representative will contact you for any additional information needed for the application.

- [ ] Documents you may need for application include your SS card or number, proof of age (such as a birth certificate), proof of citizenship status, proof of income and resources, work history, medical records, and other documents. For a full list, contact your local SS office.

- [ ] If you are unable to complete the application on your own, you are welcome to appoint a representative who can help you complete the application. To do this, you must complete appropriate forms appointing the representative. This form is different than selecting a representative payee.

Supplemental Nutrition Assistance Program (SNAP)

Low-income individuals and families may be eligible for government assistance with buying groceries through the Supplemental Nutrition Assistance Program, or SNAP (formerly food stamps). SNAP works with state agencies and community resources to provide nutritional information to individuals who receive SNAP benefits.

Checklist: Basics about SNAP

☐ To be eligible for SNAP, you must meet certain income and asset requirements. SNAP provides an online eligibility tool to help determine if you are eligible for the program.

☐ To receive SNAP benefits, your household must have $2,250 or less in countable resources, or $3,500 or less if at least one person is age 60 or older or has a disability. Countable assets do not include the primary home, and most states do not count one vehicle. Other assets may also be excluded.

☐ Income requirements for SNAP are based on either 100% of the federal poverty level for net income or 130% of the federal poverty level for gross income. Because it is based on the federal poverty level, the number of individuals in the household will influence the monthly income allowed.

□ The allotment received from SNAP will depend on the family's net monthly income and the number of people in the household. The allotment is calculated by subtracting 30% of the family's net monthly income from the maximum allotment for the household size.

□ To receive SNAP benefits, a member of the household must apply in person at the local state or county office or apply online by visiting the state agency's website. The household must file an application form, have a face-to-face or phone interview, and provide information related to income and expenses. An authorized representative is allowed to complete the application process if an individual from the household cannot complete the application, but the representative must be authorized in writing.

Chapter 6:
Benefits for Military Personnel and Their Families

The U.S. military and Department of Veterans Affairs (VA) provide numerous programs for military personnel, retirees, veterans, and their families. These benefits include both income benefits and health benefits, including access to VA health facilities. The details of these benefits are provided in the following checklists.

Checklist: Income benefits for military personnel

☐ **Retirement pay.** If you were in the military for 20 years or more, you are eligible to receive retirement pay from the military. The military calculates retirement pay depending on the date of enrollment, your pay while on active duty, and years of service.

☐ **Disability.** Disability payments from the VA are based on the extent of service-related injuries and are not dependent on income. Payments begin when the disability is first suffered. You likely do not qualify for VA disability if you did not sustain a service-related disability.

☐ **Veterans pensions.** Veterans pensions are available to individuals who enlisted before September 7, 1980, who have at least 90 days of active duty service, with at least one day during a wartime period. If the individual enlisted after September 7, 1980, they must have 24 months of active duty service, with at least one day during a wartime period. In addition, they must be age 65 or older, have a disability, be a patient in a nursing home receiving skilled nursing care, or be receiving SS disability or SSI benefits. The individual must also meet income and asset requirements to receive pension benefits.

☐ **Aid and Attendance for veterans.** Aid and Attendance benefits are for veterans who need daily unskilled nursing care at home or in a nursing home. These payments increase the monthly pension benefits. Services that qualify for Aid and Attendance include needing help with activities of daily living such as eating, bathing, and toileting.

☐ **Housebound veterans.** Veterans who are housebound due to a permanent disability, service-related or not, may be eligible for payments in addition to pension payments. However, housebound payments cannot be made to veterans who are receiving Aid and Attendance payments.

Checklist: Health benefits for military personnel

☐ **TRICARE.** If you are an active duty service member or retired from the military, you are eligible to receive health benefits through TRICARE, the military's healthcare program.

☐ **Access to VA facilities.** Eligible veterans with or without disabilities can receive medical services through the VA. Some veterans also receive dental services. Eight different enrollment Priority Groups establish priority for insurance enrollment that varies according to the type of service, extent of disability, and household income. Note that the VA healthcare system is infamous for its long wait times, sloppy recordkeeping, and treatment delays. Before using your VA benefits, be sure to research local VA facilities and evaluate whether the VA system meets your needs.

☐ **Armed Forces Retirement Homes.** Some retirees are eligible to live in one of two armed forces retirement homes located in Washington, D.C., and Gulfport, MS. Retirees must be at least 60 years old and must have served for at least 20 years. However, they must be able to live independently at time of admission, so they would have to enter the facility early in the course of a chronic terminal illness. In addition, they cannot have any psychiatric problems, and some individuals with terminal illnesses affecting cognitive function may display psychiatric symptoms, so they may be ineligible based on their psychiatric history.

☐ **Home and community-based services.** The VA offers multiple home and community-based services for veterans, including adult day healthcare, home-based primary care, homemaker and home health aide care, hospice and palliative care, PACE, respite care, skilled home healthcare, telehealth care, and veteran-directed care. A co-pay may be charged for some of these services, and services may not be available in all areas or for all veterans.

☐ **Long-term care options.** The VA offers short- and long-term nursing home benefits through three avenues: VA nursing homes (generally restricted to veterans who were disabled during military service), state nursing homes, and community nursing homes. VA benefits for long-term care will depend on your eligibility based on your service status, level of disability, and income. In addition, you must be enrolled in the VA standard medical benefits package to be eligible for long-term care benefits.

Checklist: Benefits for families of military personnel

☐ **TRICARE.** Eligible current spouses, widows/widowers, dependent parents, and even dependent parents-in-law of active duty or retired military personnel can receive health benefits through TRICARE.

☐ **CHAMPVA.** Spouses and children of individuals who are disabled due to a service-connected disability or who had a service-related disability at the time of death may qualify for benefits through the Civilian Health and Medical Program of the VA (CHAMPVA) if they do not qualify for TRICARE. The CHAMPVA program shares medical costs with the policy holder similar to other medical insurance plans. If you are eligible for Medicare, you must be enrolled in Medicare Part A and Part B to be eligible for CHAMPVA.

☐ **Pensions for survivors.** Un-remarried spouses and dependent children of deceased wartime veterans who also have limited incomes may be eligible for monthly pension payments. These payments are designed to bring the beneficiary's income up to a certain level, so they vary according to the person's existing income.

☐ **Dependency and Indemnity Compensation for survivors.** This program is for the un-remarried spouses and dependent children of veterans who died in the line of duty or who died related to injuries suffered in the line of duty. Parents of individuals who died in the line of duty may also be eligible for indemnity compensation.

☐ **Aid and Attendance or Housebound benefits.**
Qualified widows and widowers and dependent
children of veterans are eligible to receive Aid and
Attendance or Housebound benefits in addition to
pension or indemnity payments.

Checklist: Basics about TRICARE

☐ TRICARE is a military healthcare program to
provide insurance coverage for active duty service
members, National Guard and Reserve members,
retirees, their families, survivors, former spouses,
and others registered in the Defense Enrollment
Eligibility Reporting System. The available plans
depend on the individual's active duty status.

☐ TRICARE offers three basic plans: TRICARE
Prime, TRICARE Extra, and TRICARE Standard.
They also offer TRICARE for Life, which provides
additional coverage for individuals qualified for
Medicare (enrollment in Medicare Part A and Part
B is required). They also have special plans for
National Guard members, retired National Guard
members, and their families.

☐ Most individuals with a terminal illness who qualify
for TRICARE will be retired service members who
are over the age of 65 and on Medicare. Therefore,
TRICARE for Life will likely be the service
plan selected.

☐ For individuals eligible to participate in TRICARE
for Life, enrollment is not necessary and there are
no premiums (however, the individual must still
pay Part B premiums). Services covered by
TRICARE have no annual deductible, and for
active duty families or families using TRICARE
Reserve Select there is a $1,000 catastrophic cap per

family per year for covered medical expenses. For all other families, the catastrophic cap is $3,000 under Group A and $3,655 under Group B.

☐ Through their various plans, TRICARE provides medical and hospital coverage for medically necessary services, prescription coverage, dental services, vision services, preventive services, health screenings, and mental health care.

☐ TRICARE primarily uses military healthcare professionals and facilities for services, but these military healthcare services are supported by civilian services as needed.

☐ For more information about TRICARE, visit the TRICARE website.

Credit: Monkey Business Images

If you believe you qualify for military or veteran's benefits, you should contact your local VA office or visit the VA website.

Chapter 7:
Managing Medical Bills

No matter the type or level of resources available to you, paying for healthcare can be daunting. The healthcare system is bewildering and complex, and it is hard for consumers to really know the full cost of their care. For example, a patient may receive a bill for a procedure that they thought was covered by their insurance. Another patient may be unable to determine the relative costs of receiving care from different providers. A provider may be unwilling or unable to fully disclose the costs of care or provide up-front estimates. Providers may accidentally bill for services that were not rendered, and it may be difficult for patients to know that they are being overcharged in these cases.

Transparency in Medical Billing

Transparency in the cost of healthcare means making the real price of care apparent to healthcare consumers. The goal of transparency in medical costs is to give patients—the consumers—the same kind of information that is available when they shop for products like groceries. Consumers can easily reference prices at the supermarket, and they can, with a little effort, know how expensive specific items are at different stores. Transparency in medical costs aims to give healthcare consumers an easy way to determine exactly how much the care they need will cost with different providers to help them make educated choices about where they should spend their money. Transparency also involves letting consumers know the full costs of the services and items they need.

As part of its efforts to enhance patients' ability to make informed decisions about care costs, the American Medical

Association (AMA) has outlined eight ways to increase transparency in healthcare prices.

Checklist: AMA recommendations for healthcare price transparency

☐ Require all healthcare providers and entities to make information about prices for common procedures or services readily available to consumers.

☐ Ensure that physicians communicate information about the cost of their professional services to individual patients, taking into consideration patients' insurance status.

☐ Mandate that health plans provide plan enrollees or their designees with complete information regarding plan benefits and cost-sharing information in real time.

☐ Coordinate health plans, public and private entities, and other stakeholder groups to work together to facilitate price and quality transparency for patients and physicians.

☐ Enact processes to ensure the accuracy and relevance of information provided by price transparency tools.

☐ Support and strengthen all-payer claims databases.

☐ Ensure that vendors of electronic health records include features that facilitate price transparency for physicians and patients.

☐ Address patient confusion and lack of health literacy by developing resources that help them understand the complexities of healthcare pricing, and encourage them to seek information about the cost of services they receive or anticipate receiving.

In recent years, the U.S. federal government has taken steps to increase healthcare price transparency for consumers. These include the following measures.

Checklist: Government steps to increase healthcare price transparency

- ☐ In October 2018, President Trump signed two bills into law—the Know the Lowest Price Act and the Patients' Right to Know Drug Prices Act—that remove pharmacy gag clauses that prevented pharmacists from informing consumers if their prescription would cost less paid out of pocket than through their insurance plan.

- ☐ The Centers for Medicare and Medicaid Services (CMS) hospital price transparency rule went into effect on January 1, 2019, requiring hospitals to make their chargemasters publicly available. A chargemaster lists all services and items for which a hospital charges, describing the costs of these services and items in detail and disclosing any associated fees such as room charges.

- ☐ The CMS also released a resource called a Procedure Price Lookup. This tool enables patients to look up a procedure they are planning to have and compare the national average price for that procedure in both ambulatory surgical centers and hospital outpatient departments, and to see how much they will pay with an Original Medicare and no supplement (Medigap) policy.

- ☐ In November 2019, the Trump administration finalized the policies in an executive order mandating disclosure of prices throughout the healthcare industry. This will be enforceable by federal agencies and is intended to provide both patients and employers with pricing data that reflect the negotiated rates between insurers, hospitals, and physicians. It is scheduled to go into effect in January 2021.

Achieving transparency is an ongoing, complicated process. CMS administrator Seema Varna admitted in January of 2019 that CMS has no means of enforcing its transparency rule for hospital prices, there are no penalties for noncompliance, and CMS does not know how many hospitals are actually complying with the rule. Many powerful interests are involved in the issue of transparency and the costs of care are burdensome for many reasons, which makes absolute transparency difficult to achieve. However, it is likely that some kind of action toward increasing transparency will be taken in the near future.

Checking Medical Bills for Errors

The problems associated with medical billing transparency make checking medical bills for accuracy absolutely essential. Medical bills are never pleasant to receive, and it can be difficult to determine whether they are correct. If you receive a large and unexpected bill, take the time to examine it carefully. If you suspect all or part of a bill was issued in error, you can request a copy of your medical records to verify whether the bill is incorrect. Reviewing a bill in this way is your right; be prepared, however, for the comparison of your record and your bill to take a substantial amount of time. In many circumstances, you may not need to go to these lengths. If the bill is for a relatively uncomplicated visit during which you received a specific diagnosis or treatment, it may be easy to clear up the issue without diving into your medical records.

However, if the bill is for something complicated—such as a hospital stay during which you received multiple tests and procedures—then the charges may be complex. No matter the situation, if you believe you have been billed in error, remain patient, talk to your provider's billing department, and have a face-to-face meeting with someone who can explain everything to you in detail.

Medical billing is a multi-step process that begins when your provider documents diagnoses and treatments in your electronic health record (EHR). Medical billing specialists and coders—who your provider may employ directly or hire as contractors—go through a process known as abstracting in order to code procedures. This means they go through the physician's documentation to determine what elements of your visit have charges associated with them. They then assign codes to these elements and arrange the codes in order of their priority. The codes are then submitted for payment on a billing claim.

The insurance company examines the claim that is submitted to determine whether it is valid and free from errors. The insurance company then pays their portion of the bill and you are billed for the remaining balance. If you are responsible for a deductible, copay, or coinsurance, you pay that amount. If you received a diagnosis or treatment that your insurer does not cover, you may have to pay the entire bill. When errors occur during the billing process, you may also be expected to pay for things you should not have to pay for. The following checklist outlines the basic medical billing process from beginning to end.

Credit: mimagephotography

Checklist: Medical billing process

- ☐ The hospital (or other provider) checks the patient in. This includes gathering all of the patient's demographic data and insurance information, including payer and policy number.

- ☐ The hospital verifies insurance information and eligibility. For existing patients, this may simply involve asking whether any insurance information has changed. For new patients, the hospital must take all of the patient's insurance information and verify its accuracy by calling the insurance provider. To avoid potential problems with lack of coverage, patients should call the insurance company for pre-authorization and to double-check that a provider is in-network prior to receiving a service.

- ☐ The physician fills out an encounter form describing diagnoses and procedures provided to the patient. The form includes information like the date and place of service, and the physician's information.

- ☐ Medical coders use the encounter form to code the claim. Coders assign codes for any diagnoses and procedures the patient received. They may also use code modifiers to provide additional information.

- ☐ Billing specialists prepare the claim to go the insurance payer and ensure that it meets various compliance standards. Charges are entered for the services the patient received. The charge entries link the medical codes to the services and procedures rendered.

- ☐ The claim is transmitted to the insurance payer. The payer reviews the claim and verifies that it is free of errors. If the claim is accepted, the payer determines what portion of the bill it is responsible for and pays it. Some charges or the entire claim may be denied if the payer considers them medically unnecessary.

☐ The insurance payer submits a report to the billing specialist describing how much of the claim they will pay and why. If the specialist finds a problem with this report, any disputed parts of the claim may be appealed with the payer.

☐ The insurance payer pays their portion to the hospital, and that payment is posted to the patient's account. The hospital then bills the patient for their portion. If the insurance payer covers the entire bill, the charges to the patient are zero. Otherwise, the patient must pay their portion.

The checklist below outlines some of the more common medical billing errors. The majority of these errors occur on the provider side.

Checklist: Common medical billing errors

☐ Incorrect patient information, which can lead to a rejected claim and the full charge coming to the patient.

☐ Incorrect operation and/or anesthesia times, which can lead to overbilling if the times coded and billed are higher than the actual times.

☐ Miscoding, such as mismatched treatment and diagnosis codes or inaccurate diagnosis codes, which can lead the insurer to deem a procedure medically unnecessary.

☐ Upcoding, in which a diagnosis, service, or procedure is coded as more severe than it actually is, resulting in it being billed at a higher rate.

☐ Unbundling, in which services, procedures, or supplies are billed separately when they should be billed together using a single code at a package rate. For example, the hospital might bill for supplies that should be included in the room charge.

☐ Balance billing, in which you are charged for an outstanding balance after you've paid your deductible, copay, or coinsurance and the insurance company has covered its portion. The balance you're being charged in this case is the amount not covered in the price negotiated between the insurance company and the provider. The legality of this depends on whether the provider is in-network (in which case, it is usually illegal) or out-of-network (in which case, it is usually allowed).

☐ Duplicate billing, in which you are billed multiple times for the same service or procedure. This can happen if more than one person (both a doctor and a nurse, for example) document that you received a particular service.

☐ Billing for services never rendered, such as canceled tests or procedures that were never actually received. You may also be billed for drugs that were never prescribed or for which the prescriptions were canceled before you received the drugs.

If you think you've been billed in error, what should you do? The checklist below takes you through some basic steps that can help you identify and address errors in your medical bill.

Checklist: Determining whether your bill is in error and responding to an erroneous bill

☐ Don't panic. A large, unexpected bill is frightening, but you can figure it out. Try to remain calm while examining your bill. Be methodical and look at every piece of information the bill contains.

☐ Make sure you have the right bill. For example, you may receive multiple bills for the same procedure. A summary bill tells you the lump sum that you owe, but it does not itemize the charges. Do not pay this bill. If you did not receive an itemized bill, call the billing department and request a full statement with an itemized list of charges. Hospitals typically do not send an itemized bill unless you request it; take the time to request the itemized bill.

☐ Look for basic errors. Is personal information like your name and address listed correctly? Is the date and time information correct? Is your provider, policy number, group number, and other health insurance information listed correctly? All of these should be correct. A simple typo in this information could cause a claim to be rejected.

☐ Go through the bill line by line and review each item for accuracy. Make sure that every charge listed is for something you actually received. Be sure, too, that you aren't charged for something more times than it was actually done.

☐ Compare your explanation of benefits (EOB) from the hospital against your bill and your insurance plan to see if any of the charges look wrong. The EOB will tell you:

o   When you received what services

o   The medical bill charges

o   What your insurance covered

o   How much money your insurer considers to be reasonable and customary

o   How much went toward your deductible, copay, or coinsurance

o   How much money you might owe

☐   Make a list of any items in your bill that don't look correct.

☐   Contact the hospital or other provider when you are ready to discuss your concerns. Ideally, you should meet face to face with a billing representative. If the result of this meeting is that you agree to pay the charges, you can negotiate a payment plan rather than paying everything in a lump sum. You may also be able to talk the hospital down to a lower charge. Remain civil and diplomatic during the meeting, and negotiate carefully.

☐   If this process is overwhelming, consider hiring a medical billing advocate. For a fee, this person will go through your bill with you and then work with the hospital or other provider to contest errors and negotiate a better payment situation. The insurance payer may also advocate for your case because they don't want to pay erroneous charges either.

If the insurance company did not cover services that you believe they should have, you can contest their decision. The proper way to do this should be listed in your policy. Be sure to look carefully at your EOB to build the case that particular charges should be covered. For example, if your plan covers in-network diagnostic tests and you received a diagnostic test in-network but your insurer believes the test was out of network, the EOB should provide clarification. If the EOB does not support your assertion that the test was in-network, it may be that the test was coded incorrectly.

Bankruptcy and Medical Bills

Even with careful management of medical spending and diligent checking of medical bills, it is possible that medical bankruptcy is something you might face if your health insurance and personal savings cannot absorb the costs of care. Each year, an estimated 530,000 families file bankruptcy when medical bills overwhelm them, and research suggests that more than 65% of all bankruptcies are tied to medical issues. The average cost of individual healthcare for Americans was more than $10,000 annually in 2016, and that amount is expected to climb to almost $15,000 annually by 2023. While the growth of healthcare spending has slowed somewhat in the past couple years, it still continues to rise. According to HealthCare.gov, fixing a broken leg can cost up to $7,500, the average cost of a 3-day hospital stay is around $30,000, and comprehensive cancer care can cost hundreds of thousands of dollars.

Bankruptcy is a way of wiping the slate clean by discharging most types of debt. It also helps you reorganize your debt and prevents creditors from proceeding with collection activities such as foreclosure, repossession, and lawsuits. If you find yourself overwhelmed with medical debt, you may be considering this option. The checklist below describes facts to keep in mind regarding bankruptcy for medical costs.

Checklist: Bankruptcy facts for medical issues

☐ "Medical bankruptcy" is a term that refers to filing bankruptcy to escape overwhelming medical debt, but it is not an actual legal term. If you file bankruptcy because of medical debt, the bankruptcy will apply not only to your medical debt but to other kinds of unsecured, dischargeable debt as well.

☐ In addition to medical debt, unsecured, dischargeable debt includes credit card debt, personal loans, and old utility bills. Bankruptcy eliminates all of these debts.

☐ Filing for bankruptcy separates your debts into two categories—dischargeable and nondischargeable debt. Bankruptcy can eliminate dischargeable debt. It cannot eliminate nondischargeable debt, which receives priority treatment.

☐ Priority debts that cannot be discharged through bankruptcy must be paid in full through the plan. Examples of priority debts are alimony and child support, student debt (unless you can prove undue hardship in paying it back), recent tax obligations, and debt obtained by fraud.

☐ You will need to continue paying back secured debts (in which creditors have the right to take back collateral if you stop making payments on your obligation) after the bankruptcy case is over. Secured debts include car loans and mortgages.

There are two types of bankruptcy that can eliminate medical debt, Chapter 7 and Chapter 13. Both of these are known as consumer bankruptcies. Only individuals and married couples can file for these bankruptcies. Consumers are eligible for one type of bankruptcy or the other based on their income level. The following checklists provide details about these two types of bankruptcy.

Checklist: Information about Chapter 7 and Chapter 13 bankruptcy

Chapter 7 bankruptcy basics

- ☐ Chapter 7 is straight bankruptcy and is more common than Chapter 13. Chapter 7 is meant to protect lower-income earners from being swallowed by debt.

- ☐ The Chapter 7 process lasts four to six months and ideally leads to forgiveness of dischargeable debt.

- ☐ In Chapter 7, you can keep your property only if you can claim an exemption on it. Exemption rules vary by state.

- ☐ For nonexempt property, the court appoints a trustee to sell the property and distribute the proceeds from the sale to your creditors.

- ☐ There is no upper limit to the amount of debt you can discharge through a Chapter 7 bankruptcy, but you must qualify for Chapter 7 by passing a means test. The means test requires that disposable income be below a certain amount. In other words, you must make below a certain amount of money to qualify for Chapter 7. If your income is below your state's median income level, you pass the means test. Family size is taken into account. The test looks at your average income for the six months prior to filing for bankruptcy.

- Chapter 7 bankruptcy can discharge medical debt entirely, but it ruins your credit score, takes away credit cards, takes away nonexempt property, and makes it nearly impossible to secure a mortgage. Bankruptcy can remain on your record for as long as ten years.

Chapter 13 bankruptcy basics

- Chapter 13 bankruptcy is also known as reorganization bankruptcy or a wage earner's plan. If your income is too high to qualify for Chapter 7 bankruptcy, Chapter 13 is an option.

- In Chapter 13, you are given a repayment plan of three to five years for missed payments of secured debts and any nondischargeable debts that you owe. At the conclusion of the plan, your debts are discharged. Payment plans are based on your amount of disposable income and the debts that you owe.

- Creditors receive a percentage of what they are owed after you have paid all priority and secured debts. The percentage—which can range from 0% to 100%—depends on how much of your disposable income is left after you have paid priority and secured debts. At the end of your payment plan, you could potentially pay far less of your dischargeable debt than you owe.

- An automatic stay prevents lenders from foreclosing on or repossessing your property as long as you continue making payments.

- For dischargeable debts, you catch up on arrears by making small monthly payments on your debts over the plan period. For secured debts, you must make your ongoing payments while catching up on your arrears. If you do not, lenders may file a motion for relief from the stay and may receive court permission to foreclose on or repossess your property.

☐ Consequences of a Chapter 13 bankruptcy are similar to those for a Chapter 7. There are also multiple rules about filing Chapter 13 bankruptcy after filing Chapter 7 and vice versa. These rules depend on factors like the amount of time that has passed between filings and whether a previous filing was rejected. Before proceeding, make certain you are eligible to file and that you are willing to accept all the consequences of a bankruptcy.

Filing for Chapter 7

☐ Expect the process to take four to six months.

☐ Hire a reliable, experienced bankruptcy attorney. Don't try to go it alone; the process demands a lot of paperwork that can be very complicated. An attorney is an extra expense, but it is a necessary one for most people. Attorney fees for a Chapter 7 case vary according to the case's complexity and typically range from $500 to $3,500.

☐ Attend credit counseling with an approved agency to determine whether you actually need to file bankruptcy.

☐ File a petition with your local bankruptcy court. This puts the automatic stay into effect.

☐ About 30 days after you file, attend a meeting with your creditors that is presided over by your court-appointed bankruptcy trustee. The trustee may object to property you want the right to retain.

Creditors may also file suit for debts they don't want to be discharged in the bankruptcy.

☐ After filing, attend additional counseling to help you manage your finances.

Filing for Chapter 13

☐ Expect the process to take three to five years.

☐ As with a Chapter 7 bankruptcy, find and hire a knowledgeable and competent bankruptcy attorney. Most courts have guideline fees for Chapter 13 cases that attorneys are not allowed to exceed. Guideline fees vary by judicial district but typically range from $2,500 to $6,000, depending on whether you are an employee or have your own business.

☐ Complete a credit counseling course.

☐ File the bankruptcy petition and your proposed repayment plan. After you file, the automatic stay takes effect.

☐ Make your first plan payment.

☐ Attend the meeting of creditors hosted by your court-appointed bankruptcy trustee, and attend the confirmation hearing.

☐ File or object to proofs of claim.

☐ Complete the payment plan.

☐ Complete a personal financial management class.

Chapter 8:
Staying Healthy

One major cost savings that people tend to discount when considering medical costs is maintaining their personal health. Preventive measures are among the best ways to stay healthy and avoid medical expenses. Eating a healthy diet, exercising regularly, and reducing stress can all yield long-term benefits for health.

Eating a Healthy Balanced Diet

In order to have a balanced diet, you should have a daily mix of whole grains, protein, fruits, vegetables, dairy products, and different types of oils. Each of these food groups should be consumed every day in different amounts, but because they are such broad groups you still have a lot of options. The following checklist discusses some tips for consuming a balanced diet with essential nutrients.

Checklist: Tips for a balanced diet

- ☐ **Grains.** Daily grain consumption should be an even mix between refined grains and whole grains. If your daily recommended grain consumption is 6 ounces, then 3 of those ounces should be whole grains, such as whole wheat pasta, brown rice, or buckwheat products.

- ☐ **Protein.** Daily protein consumption can be satisfied with several different types of foods, including lean meats, eggs, beans, fish, seafood, soy products, and nuts and seeds.

☐ **Fruits.** A variety of fruit types should be consumed to get the most nutrients. Raw fruits generally have more nutritional value than fruit juices.

☐ **Vegetables.** When choosing vegetables, they should be a mix of red, orange, green, and starchy vegetables.

☐ **Dairy.** Dairy products can include milk, cheese, yogurt, ice cream, and sour cream. Low-fat or fat-free dairy products are healthier than dairy products containing fat, because much of the fat in dairy products is saturated fat. In addition, the calcium contained in dairy products is more readily absorbed in the presence of vitamin D.

☐ **Oils.** Oils, while not a food group, are an important part of a healthy diet because they provide essential nutrients. Olive oil is a healthier oil to cook with than vegetable oil or butter. Solid fats, such as lard, butter, and bacon grease, are much less healthy to cook with than most oils.

The nutritional information included on most food products is based on a 2,000 calorie per day diet, but this is not always the healthiest option for all individuals. For example, those who are not very physically active during the day—getting less than 30 minutes of exercise—may only need 1,600 or 1,800 calories per day. Women generally need fewer calories per day than men. While some people may need less than 2,000 per day to maintain a healthy weight or lose excess weight, others may need 2,400 or even 2,600 calories per

Credit: Shutterstock

132

day to prevent abnormal weight loss. This is generally true of individuals who are active more than 60 minutes per day and currently have a healthy weight range or individuals who have a metabolic disorder that causes unwanted weight loss. One way to determine how many calories you should consume each day is to check an online food plan generator, like the one at ChooseMyPlate, a government resource sponsored by the USDA. Generators such as this ask for your current weight, height, age, and activity level and then suggest a healthy calorie range based on these factors. People with health concerns or special dietary needs should consult with their doctor about any changes in their regular dietary habits. The following checklist provides the suggested daily amounts for each food group based on different calorie requirements.

Checklist: Daily nutrition

1,600 Calorie Diet

- ☐ Grains: 5 ounces
- ☐ Fruit: 1 ½ cups
- ☐ Vegetables: 2 cups
- ☐ Dairy: 2 ½ cups
- ☐ Protein: 5 ounces

1,800 Calorie Diet

- ☐ Grains: 6 ounces
- ☐ Fruit: 1 ½ cups
- ☐ Vegetables: 2 ½ cups
- ☐ Dairy: 3 cups

□   Protein: 5 ounces

2,000 Calorie Diet

□   Grains: 6 ounces

□   Fruit: 2 cups

□   Vegetables: 2 ½ cups

□   Dairy: 3 cups

□   Protein: 5 ½ ounces

2,200 Calorie Diet

□   Grains: 7 ounces

□   Fruit: 2 cups

□   Vegetables: 3 cups

□   Dairy: 3 cups

□   Protein: 6 ounces

Portion size is very important when considering a balanced diet. Many people do not realize how small portion sizes should be in order to adhere to particular calorie requirements. For example, a hamburger that contains a quarter pound of meat—the typical size of a small hamburger—is four ounces of protein. For a 2,000 calorie a day diet, that one hamburger makes up almost your entire allotment of protein for the day. The amount of food that is served at restaurants is often much greater than the recommended daily amounts. Consider a typical steak dinner at a restaurant. Normally, steaks served at restaurants are between 6 and 12 ounces and come with sides ranging from potatoes and cooked vegetables to a serving of French fries. If you eat the whole steak, you could actually consume up to twice the amount of protein recommended for the day and a large portion of saturated fat as well. If a baked potato is served with the meal, that is approximately 1 cup or more from your vegetable requirement for the day, and if you add butter and sour cream to your potato, you are again increasing saturated fat consumption. If you also have cooked vegetables on the side, you could get close to 2 cups of vegetables in one meal. All of this is not even including any appetizers, bread, or dessert that was served with the meal. Many restaurants are now required to have calorie counts listed on the menu, so portions are a bit easier to estimate, but it is still good practice to consider how much is being consumed when working to achieve a balanced diet.

Consuming a balanced diet allows your body to function at optimal health. Operating at optimal health essentially means that your whole body benefits—including your brain. Foods that are high in sugar or fat slow down brain activity because they eventually lead to high insulin levels. When the high insulin levels begin to recede, a "sugar crash" occurs, in which you begin to feel sluggish, tired, and unable to process information as quickly as before. If these "crashes" occur frequently, they can cause physical, lasting damage to the memory centers of your brain.

Consuming a balanced diet helps eliminate chances for further damage by supplying the brain with nutrients needed to function at optimal capacity and protect against any harmful chemicals or cell degeneration. A balanced and healthy diet can also help moderate body weight, especially when combined with daily exercise. Engaging in daily physical activities will not only help ensure a healthy body weight, but it can also help prevent disease.

Individuals who live in the Mediterranean region have higher life expectancies than most populations and have a lower rate of individuals with dementia. The main component of this dietary approach is eating large portions of fruits, vegetables, whole grains, and legumes. Most, if not all, meals should be made up of these ingredients, with approximately six or more servings of fruits and vegetables per day. In addition, whole grains are very important and should be included in most meals. Fish and seafood are another essential component of this diet, providing protein and omega 3s. Most who follow the Mediterranean diet consume fish or seafood at least twice a week, if not more frequently. Conversely, red meat should be eaten infrequently, no more than once or twice per month. Poultry, such as chicken and turkey, can be eaten in place of red meat. In addition to limiting consumption of red meat, the Mediterranean diet also suggests avoiding butter, salt, high-fat dairy products, and refined sugars.

Another popular diet, the Whole 30 diet, argues that certain food groups such as sugar, grains, dairy, and legumes negatively affect your health and fitness. The Whole 30 diet promotes eating foods with very few ingredients, all pronounceable ingredients, or whole foods with no ingredients listed at all; moderate portions of meat, seafood, and eggs; lots of vegetables; some fruit; natural fats; and herbs, spices, and seasonings. The idea behind this diet is to—for 30 days—avoid eating problem foods such as junk food, dairy, legumes, grains, and sugar and to avoid consuming alcohol. This is promoted as a kind of detoxification process to make a conclusive break with unhealthy patterns of dietary consumption.

Whether you embrace diets such as these is something you should discuss with your primary care physician. Discuss the diet plan you want to try. Your physician may have concerns or may have specific recommendations for how you should best implement the plan safely and healthily. Your physician may also refer you to resources that you should consult before embarking on any new diet plan.

Getting Exercise

Some people hear the word exercise and immediately think of running, jogging, or other activities that are not always considered enjoyable by the majority of people. However, exercise can be any physical activity that you enjoy doing that increases your heart rate. If you do not like running, or if it is physically painful for you, then consider another activity such as swimming, biking, or walking. You are much more likely to stick with an exercise routine if you enjoy the activity. Similarly, it could be helpful to find a friend to exercise with, as this will encourage both of you to continue exercising. You and your friend, or group of friends, could plan to go to the gym a few times a week or plan to take a half hour walk each night. Setting up a regular schedule and including another person in your exercise routine can help make it more enjoyable. Creating goals can also increase your motivation. These goals should be attainable; if you set an unrealistic goal, then you will feel defeated when you do not succeed. Instead, begin with small, attainable goals, and be proud of yourself when you meet them. This success will then help you continue to meet larger exercise goals that you set as time goes on.

Typically, individuals who try to incorporate regular or daily exercise into their routines stop after a week or two, especially if they do not particularly enjoy exercising. If you can stick with an exercise routine for a month, the likelihood of it becoming a habit increases substantially. Creating a habit takes approximately 28 days, at which point the activity becomes routine. If you can commit to 30 minutes of moderate physical activity—such as walking or gardening—for 28 days, the activity will be much easier to continue, because it will become part of your daily routine.

Although exercise in most forms is considered to be beneficial, some high-impact sports—such as football, hockey, boxing, and rugby—have an increased risk of head injury. Repeated head injuries can cause damage to the brain. Be careful and wear appropriate protective gear when engaging in these sports. Similarly, if you choose to exercise by riding a bike or skating, always make sure to wear a safety helmet in case of falls.

The checklist below outlines the Department of Health and Human Services (HHS) guidelines for adult exercise. The HHS also has guidelines for older adults and adults with chronic health conditions or disabilities.

Checklist: HHS guidelines for adult exercise

☐ Move more and sit less throughout the day. Some physical activity is better than none, and any amount of moderate-to-vigorous physical activity confers some health benefits.

☐ Do at least 150 minutes to 300 minutes a week of moderate-intensity, 75 minutes to 150 minutes a week of vigorous-intensity aerobic physical activity, or an equivalent combination of moderate- and vigorous-intensity aerobic activity. Preferably, aerobic activity should be spread throughout the week instead of being crammed into just one or two days.

☐ Engage in physical activity beyond the equivalent of 300 minutes of moderate-intensity physical activity a week.

☐ Do muscle-strengthening activities of moderate or greater intensity and that involve all major muscle groups on 2 or more days a week, as these activities provide additional health benefits.

Reducing Stress

You will most effectively reduce stress if you simultaneously lessen the impact of stressors in your life and increase your ability to cope with them.

Checklist: Basics about reducing stress

- ☐ Take a break from your responsibilities for ten to twenty minutes per day and spend time in meditation or reflection. The form of your meditation can be aligned with a spiritual tradition, but it doesn't have to be. It can be as simple as taking a few moments to slow down your thoughts.

- ☐ Exercise to pour your energy into something other than your problems as well as benefit your mind and body.

- ☐ Limit screen time not related to work or school activities to two hours or less each day. Engage in physical activity instead.

- ☐ See your doctor regularly and maintain your physical health. Physical well-being is closely tied to emotional health.

- ☐ Keep active with hobbies that involve your mind and/or body, such as gardening, playing or listening to music, crafting, cooking, or reading.

- ☐ Make to-do lists to keep track of your upcoming responsibilities. Calendars and planners can help you survey your priorities at a glance.

- ☐ Avoid stressful multitasking and try to streamline your daily tasks. Trying to do too much at once just adds to your stress level.

- [ ] Understand your limits, and don't be afraid to say "no."

- [ ] Talk to friends and family regularly to have partners in coping.

- [ ] Write your thoughts out in a journal.

- [ ] Use humor to help you through stressful situations.

- [ ] When good things happen, appreciate them.

Chapter 9:
Other Money-Saving Measures

No matter your resources or your current health, there are simple things you can start doing today that could yield substantial care-related savings. Some may require a little research on your part and some may force you outside of comfortable routines, but all of them can have a positive impact for a small investment of time. This is especially true with prescription spending. The following checklist outlines a few options for saving money at the pharmacy.

Checklist: Saving money on prescriptions

☐ **Ask about generics.** Check with your doctor about the availability of generic versions of your prescriptions. Generic medications use different fillers than brand name drugs but are required by the FDA to meet the same standards of quality, strength, and purity. If generics are not available, a comparable brand name drug may be available for a lower price. Newer, pricier drugs often have the same effects as older, cheaper drugs that work through different mechanisms or have different side effects. If you can accept these differences, your wallet may benefit.

☐ **Use a mail-order pharmacy.** U.S. based mail-order pharmacies have lower overhead costs than brick-and-mortar pharmacies, and they pass those savings on to their customers. It is important, however, to do your homework before signing up with a mail-order pharmacy. Make sure the pharmacy practices and is licensed in the United States, holds a Verified Pharmacy Practice Site certification, requires a prescription to fill your order, and employs an actual pharmacist that you can speak to over the phone. If you are insured, you should check that the pharmacy is recognized by your insurance provider. Some insurers have a preferred mail-order company that they recommend you use.

☐ **Shop around brick-and-mortar pharmacies.** Comparison shopping prescriptions can take a little time, but may be worth your while if you take multiple medications or medications that are expensive. Be sure to compare the costs of chain pharmacies, local independent pharmacies, and grocery retailers with in-store pharmacies. Wholesale clubs that charge a membership fee, like Costco, may also offer prescription drugs at substantial discounts. Independent local pharmacies may be willing to negotiate with you on price, especially if you have price quotes from their competitors. If you live in a large, heavily populated city, venture outside of town to do some comparison shopping; the cost of prescriptions is often cheaper in suburban areas. Don't be afraid to break up your prescriptions—one retailer may be substantially cheaper on one prescription while another retailer is substantially cheaper on a different prescription.

☐ **Research prescription assistance programs.** Pharmaceutical companies often have prescription assistance programs or PAPs. The purpose of these programs is to help uninsured or under-insured consumers afford very high-priced prescription drugs. To apply for assistance, you need to identify the manufacturer of the costly drug, research whether it has a PAP, and determine whether you qualify to receive the drug at low- or no-cost through the program. Websites like NeedyMeds simplify this process by aggregating information about many manufacturers in a single location.

☐ **Consider pharmacy discount programs.** Some national chain pharmacies offer discount programs to individuals without prescription coverage. These programs may require a small annual fee in exchange for discounts on fills of most prescriptions. The fee is often recouped within a couple of months.

☐ **Use your flex dollars**. Many employers offer flexible spending accounts (FSAs) or health spending accounts (HSAs) to their employees. Both FSAs and HSAs allow pre-tax earnings to be set aside to pay for medical expenses, prescriptions, and some over-the-counter medical products. Depending on your tax rate, this may yield substantial savings for you. Both employers and employees can contribute to both types of accounts, and HSA dollars that are unused at the end of one year will roll over to the next year. However, FSA dollars that are unused at the end of one year do not roll over to the next year, meaning you must use those dollars or lose them.

☐ **Check into the NACo card.** The National Association of Counties—or NACo—is an affiliation of counties across the United States that supports a variety of county government initiatives. One of these initiatives is improving access to healthcare for individuals who are uninsured or who do not have prescription coverage. If you live in a participating county and qualify for the program, you may be eligible to receive a prescription card that could save you an average of 24 percent on your drug costs.

☐ **Explore local programs.** Many state and local programs are available to help consumers with healthcare costs. Most states have low- or no-cost community health centers for people who are uninsured or underinsured. These clinics may provide full medical exams and basic preventive care like vaccinations and flu shots. In large urban areas, tax-funded county hospitals may offer similar programs. Some charitable organizations also sponsor clinics; doctors at these clinics are often well-versed in identifying the least costly drugs for certain conditions and may offer vouchers for some medications. It can be difficult to find information about these programs. Good starting points for locating this information are representatives from your state's health department and social workers at local hospitals.

In addition to saving money at the pharmacy, you can look for ways to make the money you spend work harder for you. Many pharmacies and grocery retailers with in-store pharmacies offer free rewards programs. You are likely familiar with these cards; a cashier typically scans the card before ringing your purchase. This, in turn, tracks your spending and may accumulate points that you can use for money off future purchases. What you may not realize is

Credit: Shutterstock

that some retailers track pharmacy spending as well as spending on non-pharmacy items. Seeking out a pharmacy with this type of rewards program—and remembering to scan your card before every pharmacy purchase—will help you accumulate points. There may be restrictions on applying points toward future prescription purchases, but the points can be used to save money on other items in your budget like over-the-counter drugs, medical products, and groceries.

If you plan to pay for healthcare purchases—whether at the pharmacy, hospital, or elsewhere—using a personal credit card, consider using a card that offers some sort of spending rewards. Insurance premiums, prescriptions, and provider bills can usually be paid with a credit card. These types of expenditures typically do not fall into any kind of special "bonus" categories but should still be eligible for basic "non-bonus" category percentage earnings. When choosing a card, look for one with spending rewards that are most useful to you. The most common types of spending rewards are airline miles and cashback dollars. If you like to or need to travel often, an airline card may be the right answer for you; if you'd rather take money off of your credit card balance, a cashback card may be a better choice. No matter the type of reward you choose, spending rewards typically offer between one and three percent rewards on non-bonus category purchases, with bonus category purchases sometimes earning up to five percent rewards. Some cards have thresholds for earning certain levels of rewards.

Be certain to do your homework when considering bonus cards. Some cards have an annual fee, some have limitations on when and how you can redeem your spending rewards, and some offer low introductory interest rates that increase in time. In addition, make sure to use good spending practices when paying for healthcare with a credit card. If you charge more than you can pay off each month, your interest payments will quickly outweigh the benefits of your spending rewards.

Chapter 10:
Special Considerations
for Older Adults

Understanding healthcare money management is a struggle for many people, and it presents additional, unique problems for older adults. Many older adults are retired or preparing for retirement while also coping with the burdens of long-term illness. Decisions about where to retire, how to seek assistance in the community, and when to share responsibility for finances play a major role in securing quality, affordable care in your later years. It is also important to understand how to protect yourself from frauds and scams that target older adults.

Retiring Abroad

For people interested in a lower overall cost of living—along with cheaper healthcare or prescriptions—retiring abroad may be an option. Many countries outside of the United States offer more affordable lifestyle options that can help retirees stretch their savings. In many of these countries, a monthly budget of $2,000 goes a long way and may make retirees among the wealthiest members of the population.

A sizeable number of U.S. retirees are opting to move abroad. In 2016, the U.S. Social Security Administration made 400,000 payments per month to overseas retirees. That number jumped to 500,000 in 2017. Depending on location, retirees overseas enjoy lower rent; more inexpensive healthcare; cheaper locally produced groceries; and substantial over-60 discounts on utilities, taxes, and public transportation.

It is important to remember, however, that the cost of living should not be the only reason to move outside the United States. People who do so—sometimes referred to as economic refugees or economic ex-pats—may be unprepared for the differences between daily life in the United States and daily life in another country, and this can lead to disappointment. The following checklist can help you evaluate whether you are ready for retired life abroad.

Credit: Shutterstock

Checklist: Evaluating your readiness to retire abroad

☐ **Do you like adventure?** Successful retirees enjoy change and have an open mind. They don't mind when the store doesn't have the particular products they want, are not bothered when scheduled appointments are missed without warning, and are not frustrated when the Internet or phone lines go down indefinitely.

☐ **Do you have a sense of humor?** Being able to laugh off your mistakes and misinterpretations of your environment and to enjoy the idiosyncrasies of your new community are essential to success.

☐ **Is your partner onboard?** Both halves of any couple retiring abroad must be equally invested in the move in order for it to work. If one partner is enthusiastic about the move and the other is merely tolerant, the change is unlikely to be successful.

☐ **Do you have a return plan?** Even if you believe that you want to move permanently, be prepared that you may return to the United States at some point. Changes in your health or that of family members, changes in the political climate in your new country, and simple homesickness for people and places in the United States may dictate that it is time to go.

Before you select a retirement destination, you must be honest with yourself about what you need and want in your retirement and about what you can and cannot live without. Life in the United States is full of conveniences that are simply not part of life in many other countries. Other cultures have different laws and different societal norms that can vary greatly from those in the United States. Retirees abroad must be prepared for these realities and must be willing to embrace them in order for their move to be successful. Constant comparisons between the United States and your new home will lead to disappointment.

When deciding if retiring abroad is right for you, it is a good idea to determine your must-haves and your must-not-haves. This will help you not only analyze your wishes but narrow down potential retirement destinations. The following checklist provides some ideas about things you may and may not want in selecting your new home.

Checklist: Must-have and must-not-have items for retiring abroad

- ☐ Quality healthcare

- ☐ Low cost of living

- ☐ Large English-speaking population

- ☐ Large American community

- ☐ Quality public transportation (ability to live without a car)

- ☐ Numerous travel options for returning to the United States

- ☐ Reliable and fast phone and Internet access

- ☐ Stable, non-violent political and social climate

- ☐ Lack of social stratification

- ☐ Religious tradition in keeping with your own or that is not in direct opposition to your own

- ☐ Sanitary conditions similar to the United States

Once you've identified your priorities for living, investigate locations. This will require research on your part. Online research can be a good place to start, and the recent trend for retiring abroad has given rise to a number of useful sites. Do not be afraid to peruse blogs by ex-pat retirees as well; while these may not be reliable sources of information about legal matters, they can provide interesting insights into day-to-day life and individual struggles with things like language barriers, securing healthcare, and finding a place to live. The following checklist gives some of the most popular countries for retiring abroad.

Checklist: Popular countries for retiring abroad

- ☐ Colombia

- ☐ Costa Rica

- ☐ Malaysia

- ☐ Malta

- ☐ Mexico

- ☐ Panama

- ☐ Portugal

☐   Spain

☐   Thailand

After zeroing in on potential locations, visit them. It is best to do so during low tourism seasons in order to see what the locations truly have to offer. This will give you a chance to get an understanding of the weather, the accessibility of food and services, and the general pace and routine of life in the area. When making these trips, do your best to live like a local rather than a tourist: rent a house or apartment rather than staying in a resort, do your own cooking rather than dining out, and try getting a haircut or visiting a laundromat. Do these things using the type of transportation you would be likely to use if you lived there—take a bicycle, walk, or use public transportation if that's what the locals do rather than renting a car or taking a taxi. This will help you understand whether you can cope with riding home from the store with two bags of groceries in your bike basket. Visit the hospital, pharmacy, and local bank to see if you are comfortable with what they have to offer. If possible, extend your stay for several weeks rather than just a few days.

Be sure to consider the legal aspects of moving early in the process. Residency may not be an option in some countries. For example, Australia and New Zealand have very strict requirements for foreign residents that may make living there infeasible. Other countries welcome retirees interested in relocation. A number of countries—particularly in South America—offer special visas to individuals of retirement age. Often, these programs require proof of monthly income of roughly $1,000—an amount that is easily covered by many retirees' Social Security income. Remember, too, that there will likely be fees associated with securing a visa, and the process may necessitate hiring an attorney in the country in which you are seeking residency. The following checklist outlines other costs to consider when moving abroad.

Checklist: Costs to consider when moving abroad for retirement

☐ **Your home and possessions in the United States.** If you choose not to sell your home, you will still be responsible for upkeep, maintenance, and insurance. Renting the home may generate enough income to cover these expenses, but may necessitate hiring a property management company. Also, storing a car or any other belongings that you are not taking with you will generate additional costs.

☐ **Your utility bills in your new location.** Wi-fi, electricity, and fuel can cost far more outside of the United States. Be sure to research local costs for these things before moving in order to build your budget accordingly.

☐ **The cost of doing business in English.** If you move to a country where the primary language is not English, you will likely pay extra for services. In some cases, it may simply be the practice of restaurant or store owners to charge higher prices to non-native speakers (under the assumption that they are tourists rather than locals). In other cases—such as calling a plumber—additional charges may apply if you request an individual who speaks English. This charge is reflective of the difficulty business owners have in securing skilled employees who are also proficient in English.

☐ **Fees inherent in governmental systems.** Some processes that are quite cheap and simple in the United States are more expensive and complicated in other countries. This may include getting a driver's license, getting a tax ID, and applying for residency. There will be extra costs if you require a broker, consultant, lawyer, or translator to aid in the process.

☐ **Local health insurance costs.** While healthcare is considerably cheaper in many locations than it is in the United States, you will still need to purchase health insurance and premiums may be among your largest expenses. Medicare coverage does not extend outside of the United States and you may be ineligible for national insurance in your new country. Even if you are eligible for national insurance, it may not be the most economically feasible option. In this case, you will need to purchase private insurance.

☐ **Exchange rate fluctuations.** Depending on where you move, the exchange rate can be costly. In less developed countries, the rate will likely work in your favor. In countries with strong currencies, the rate will likely work against you. Keep in mind the importance of long-range fluctuations—an exchange rate that is favorable when you first move may no longer work in your favor after five years.

☐ **Costs of homesickness.** You will likely need or want to travel back to the United States at least once each year, and that expense must be built into your budget. It is also wise to plan on an extra trip back once in a while when special circumstances necessitate it. Be aware, too, that the desire for certain items from home can get costly. For example, if you must have a certain brand of cookies, anticipate the extra cost associated with obtaining them and budget accordingly.

Many of these costs can be minimized with a bit of upfront planning. It is a good idea to enlist the help of a financial planner as you begin planning for your move abroad, particularly one who has worked with ex-pat retirees in the past. Some additional money-saving tips are covered in the following checklist.

Checklist: Money-saving tips for retiring abroad

☐ Rent property rather than buying it. In many countries, it is difficult or impossible for foreigners or individuals without earned income to secure a mortgage. In addition, it can be risky to enter into long-term financial contracts in a foreign language. Renting helps you avoid these problems and increases your flexibility in the event you decide to return to the United States or move to a different country.

☐ Keep the majority of your money in the United States. U.S. banks are federally insured and may be more stable than banks abroad. Direct deposit of 401(k) and IRA distributions should be made into stateside accounts rather than foreign accounts to avoid a 10% withholding tax. If you move to a country that relies heavily on cash transactions, you will need to make sure that you can access your funds through ATMs with low or no fees. If you must open a local account, do not plan to move all of your funds to that account. Social Security income can be directly deposited to an account at a foreign bank without penalties or extra taxes.

☐ Leave your investments with U.S. firms. Foreign-based mutual funds tend to be more expensive than those in the United States, and buying and selling securities outside of the United States can create tax issues. Make sure there is a way for you to manage any U.S.-based investments electronically when you are outside of the country.

☐ Get a credit card that does not charge a foreign transaction fee. Cards with fees typically charge 1% to 3% on all purchases made outside of the United States, and that can add up quickly if you are living in a country that relies heavily on credit card transactions. If possible, find a card that gives you travel rewards to help cover the costs of trips back and forth to the United States.

☐ Understand your tax status. The United States bases taxation on citizenship rather than residency, and it is the only major country that does so. This is especially costly for individuals living abroad while earning large salaries; it is less costly for retirees because they typically do not generate much, if any, income abroad. However, you must still pay both U.S. taxes and local taxes for the country in which you reside. In most cases, any local tax you pay can be credited on your U.S. tax return; this means that you will not face double taxation. In addition, you will have to file additional paperwork if you maintain more than $10,000 in foreign bank accounts. It may be helpful to hire an accountant who has experience working with retirees abroad.

☐ Know the residency requirements. Some countries are very welcoming of retirees and have easy, relatively inexpensive visa processes. Other countries have lengthy, expensive processes. Living in a retiree-friendly country can reduce the amount you must pay to secure the paperwork you need to remain in the country.

Community Assistance

Whether you opt to retire abroad or to remain stateside, many local community organizations provide low-cost

Credit: Monkey Business Images

services to retirees. These services may include meal delivery, transportation, and care facilitation. Each community has a different set of programs, so you may need to do some research into what resources are available in your area.

Checklist: Types of community assistance

☐ Adult day care centers

☐ Advice on financial considerations and assistance

☐ Advice on legal matters

☐ Caregiver support

☐ Counseling and support groups

☐ Crisis intervention

☐ Education workshops

☐ Elder care consulting and advocacy

☐ Housing or rental assistance

☐ Meal assistance

☐ Medical information

☐ Respite care for caregivers

☐ Subsidies for home care

☐ Transportation

☐ Utility assistance

Checklist: How to find low-cost community resources

☐ Search online for your state's Department of Aging, Elder Affairs, or Senior Services. These agencies provide state-specific information and resources.

☐ Search your city's government sites for community resources provided for medically or financially needy individuals.

☐ Search online for charitable organizations in your area that may provide services or resources for people with your specific needs.

☐ If you are religious, your denomination may offer low-cost services. For example, the Catholic order Little Sisters of the Poor offers nursing home services to the very poorest older people in need of care.

☐ The U.S. Administration on Aging and AARP provide information and low-cost services to millions of older Americans.

☐ Talk to family members, community leaders, friends, faith community members, and others about helping or locating low-cost care options.

☐ The National Council on Aging and Eldercare Locator provide online tools for locating community resources.

Transitioning Control of Finances

If you are an older adult with a long-term illness, you may experience a decline in cognitive function that affects your ability to make responsible financial decisions over time. If you sense this has started happening to you, or if you anticipate that it will be a likely consequence of your illness, you should begin the process of transitioning control of finances to a durable power of attorney as soon as possible.

If cognitive decline from terminal illness occurs, it tends to be progressive. As a result, you will be better able to participate in financial decision making early in the course of a disease, and transitioning control of your finances will be much simpler if you are able to agree to the changes your financial representative is making. If you wait too long to talk to your loved ones about transitioning financial control, you might put your finances at risk with your spending behaviors and the choices you make about insurance and medical costs. To add to this urgency, you are only able to sign power of attorney documents while you are still legally competent to do so—which is typically early in the course of diseases like Alzheimer's and other forms of dementia. If you wait until you are no longer legally competent to make the transition, your loved ones will have to go to court to be named conservator for you. This process can take several months.

My dad and I (Laura) waited too long to transition control of his finances. At the time, I lived several states away, and I did not realize how bad my dad's cognitive functioning had become. This was, in part, due to an incorrect medical diagnosis we had received. By the time I took control of Dad's finances, this is what he had done:

- Given thousands to scammers in Jamaica in hopes of winning a "lottery"

- Bought a vacation timeshare

- Loaned money to "friends" who we never heard from again

- Given thousands to the humane society (I'm all for giving to charity, but this was money he needed, and the humane society was not a cause he would have chosen had he been thinking clearly.)

– Overpaid credit cards by several hundred dollars, which then had to be refunded

– Made mistakes that cost him bank fees

I was only able to recover about 20% of the money mentioned above. In trying to recover these funds, I learned that entire networks of people prey on the sick and elderly. They even exchange databases that include names, addresses, and what they personally know about each individual. Law enforcement is overwhelmed with "more important" issues and will not spend much time helping you bring these scammers to justice. In the case of the Jamaican "lottery," I had the phone number, address, and name of the person who contacted my dad. I talked to the U.S. State Department and filled out several forms, but I never heard anything back. Government agencies do not have the funds to track down all the crooks in the world, and the amount of $2,000 was petty to them, even though it was a large amount for my father.

How can you ensure that you do not make similar costly financial mistakes? Watch yourself for signs of confusion or frustration in everyday transactions, then discuss these issues with a loved one as soon as possible so you have ample time to find a financial management strategy that works for you and your family. The following checklists will help guide you through this process, but you should also talk to a financial planner about possible solutions for your personal situation.

Checklist: Signs that it may be time to transition control of your finances

☐ You sometimes have difficulty counting change, paying for a store purchase, calculating a tip, balancing a checkbook, or understanding a bank statement.

☐ You struggle to keep your bills organized.

☐ You pay bills late, overpay, or forget to pay entirely. These mistakes can result in late fees, interruption of service, and finance charges.

☐ You sometimes have trouble determining whether a letter is a bill or junk mail.

☐ You feel overwhelmed by the volume and type of mail you receive.

☐ You feel increasingly vulnerable to scams.

☐ You have run into problems with telemarketers.

If you no longer feel capable of handling your own finances, you must find a way to discuss sharing financial responsibility with a trusted individual, take the necessary legal and financial steps for doing so, and plan for your future. Be sure to take the conversation at a pace that is appropriate to your relationship. Keep in mind that while you may be frustrated and scared about your current situation, they may also be frightened for your future. It's

Credit: Ken Tannenbaum

okay to acknowledge that the situation is difficult but that you are confident you can make the best of it together.

Checklist: How to approach a discussion about finances with your loved one

☐ Start discussions early. Talking about finances is more comfortable when it is a seemingly distant issue, and legal documents needed to transfer financial responsibility are easiest to create when you are legally competent.

☐ Ask permission to talk about financial issues, because your loved one might want to avoid the reality that you will eventually no longer have the mental capacity to manage your own finances. Be firm, however, and have the discussion, because planning is a necessity.

☐ Discuss your plan for dealing with the financial impact of your disease.

☐ Look for appropriate opportunities to begin a conversation about finances, and follow through with the discussion when the opportunity arises.

☐ Use your best judgment about whether to back off or be persistent if your loved one resists the discussion. If you back off, watch for opportunities to raise the issue again.

☐ Tell your loved one that having the discussion now and keeping up an ongoing conversation will save a lot of anxiety for both of you later. It will also ensure that your wishes are thoroughly understood and carried out.

☐ Mention that your attorney, physician, banker, or insurance representative raised the issue that finances can become complicated for people with a chronic terminal illness.

- [ ] Set a formal "appointment" to discuss financial matters, especially if an opportunity has not arisen. Meet in a private place.

- [ ] Start with a story of someone else's experience, discussing how they wished they would have had a financial plan in place or were thankful that they had such a plan.

- [ ] Focus on positive aspects of sharing financial responsibility by mentioning that your loved one will no longer have worry about whether you are keeping up on your bills and protecting yourself from scammers.

- [ ] Be calm and open, and don't try to move too fast or force the issue.

- [ ] If your loved one is dismissive of your concerns or is not responding to you, see whether a trusted relative or friend will talk to them about the importance of sharing financial control with you.

Credit: Konstantin Sutyagin

Once you have discussed your finances with your loved one, you're ready to start transitioning the management of your finances over to them. The following checklist provides information for individuals who have legal control over the finances of another person, such as a spouse or durable power of attorney for finances.

Checklist: Transitioning management of your finances to a loved one

Spouse:

- ☐ If you have a chronic terminal illness and you were the primary individual who managed finances for your household, it is usually relatively easy to legally transition control of finances to your spouse, especially if you have normally filed taxes jointly.

- ☐ Discuss with your spouse all the financial accounts that you held either jointly or separately, including bank accounts, investments, and other accounts. Hopefully, you will have done this throughout the course of your marriage, and they may already know this information even without a discussion.

- ☐ Accounts that you held jointly will need no further action, because your spouse is already listed as an owner on the account and can complete transactions for that account.

- ☐ If you have separate accounts for which your spouse is not a joint owner, they will need to be assigned co-ownership of the accounts. This process is relatively straightforward. You and your spouse simply need to go to the bank or other financial institution and you need to add your spouse as a co-owner on the account. This usually must be done in person.

- ☐ If you file taxes separately, your spouse may not want to be listed as a co-owner on any new accounts because it might affect their taxes. In addition, some accounts, such as IRAs, do not allow joint ownership. In these cases, your spouse can become a durable power of attorney or conservator for you. If you receive Social Security benefits, your spouse will need to be designated as your representative payee.

- If your spouse is power of attorney or conservator for you, your spouse will need to file the legal paperwork with each financial institution with which you have an account for which they are not a joint owner. It is usually best to file these documents in person. Financial institutions often have their own paperwork that your spouse will need to sign in addition to filing the legal documents.

- If your spouse cannot visit the financial institution in person to file legal documents, they should call and speak to someone who can give them instructions for how to file legal paperwork. That way they will know which documents the bank needs and who to send those documents to. If the bank needs to send your spouse additional paperwork to sign, that process can get started quickly.

- If you have a joint account with someone other than your spouse (e.g., a minor or adult child, former spouse, or parent), you and your spouse will need to talk to the joint owner to determine what needs to be done with that account. If the joint owner is not willing to let your spouse manage the account on your behalf, you may need to relinquish control of the account to the joint owner. However, if your spouse is power of attorney or conservator for you, they already have legal access to the account as long as they file the correct paperwork with the financial institution.

- If you normally file taxes separately, it may be beneficial to start filing taxes jointly. Many of the government programs that provide financial assistance have much more favorable financial requirements for couples who file taxes jointly compared to those who file taxes separately.

☐ Once your spouse has legal access to manage your financial accounts, you will need to discuss your household budget to make sure all bills are paid on time and correctly. This may also include regular charitable donations that you give.

☐ You will need to notify any companies that require your financial information, such as utility companies, credit card companies, and insurance companies, that your spouse will now be managing the account. Again, if you are both already listed as account owners, you will not need to do anything further. However, if your spouse is not listed as an account owner, they will need to provide the company with the new financial information it needs.

☐ If you pay bills or manage accounts online, you will need to give login and password information to your spouse so they can manage those accounts.

Non-spouse:

☐ Although account co-ownership may be the best option if you will be transitioning financial control to your spouse, it is not usually the best option in other situations. If your loved one is co-owner of your accounts and they are not a spouse who files taxes jointly, assuming co-ownership of accounts forces them to assume half of the tax liability for those accounts. This may significantly impact your loved one's financial situation. Therefore, for someone who is not your spouse, co-ownership of accounts should be a last resort.

☐ Rather than being listed as a co-owner on accounts, your loved one should draw up legal paperwork to be your durable power of attorney or conservator. A durable power of attorney document can be drawn up with the help of an attorney before you are legally incompetent, but a conservator must be appointed by the court if you are no longer legally competent.

☐ Some government programs, such as Social Security and the VA, require their own documentation for individuals managing financial resources received from these institutions. Therefore, your loved one will need to file representative payee or VA fiduciary applications with the appropriate agency. When they are approved, they should read all documentation so they understand their responsibilities.

☐ Once the necessary legal paperwork is completed, your loved one will need to contact each financial institution or company with which you have accounts. This includes banks, investment companies, companies that manage retirement funds, credit card companies, utility companies, mortgage companies, insurance companies, and others. This may also include safe deposit boxes and titles to real estate or vehicles. If possible, legal paperwork should be filed in person and any documents that will allow your loved one to have legal control over your accounts should be completed in person. If filing in person is not possible, your loved one can call the institution or company to make arrangements to assume control of the account.

☐ If your loved one has legal control of your finances, you need to sit down with them (and your spouse, if applicable) to discuss your financial wishes. Your loved one needs to understand your budget; your normal giving, spending, and saving patterns; your tax status; your sources of income; your debts; and your other financial resources. Your loved one's goal should be to manage your finances the same way you would.

☐ If you manage any accounts online, make sure you give your loved one the login and password information so they can continue to manage those accounts. They may also need to change the email address associated with the account or gain access to your email account so they can receive important communications associated with the account.

Taking on financial responsibility for another individual is a big step. Your loved one may be overwhelmed with all the different accounts that need to be managed and updated, and understanding your financial resources and options may be confusing to them at first. The following checklist will help you and your loved one simplify your finances. Remember that the initial transfer of responsibility is the most complicated part. Once your loved one has managed your finances for a few months, it will be easier for them.

Checklist: Steps to simplify your finances when sharing control with a loved one

☐ Get monthly income sources like Social Security and pension checks directly deposited to your bank account.

☐ If you are drawing income from retirement accounts as needed, make sure your loved one understands the requirements, fees, and penalties associated with each account and knows the balance of each account. Some accounts have penalties for early withdrawals or have minimum withdrawal requirements once you reach a certain age. This will help your loved one know which accounts to draw money from first to help cover expenses.

☐ If your loved one is named as the representative payee for your Social Security benefits, they may find it easier to file their annual financial report if SS funds are kept in a separate account. These funds should be used for paying medical bills, mortgage or rent, food, and other necessary expenses. Your loved one should keep track of each transaction. If all of this money is not spent on necessary expenses each month, the remainder should be saved in an interest-bearing savings account.

☐ Arrange to have important bills paid automatically each month or mailed directly to your loved one.

☐ Cancel unnecessary credit cards, especially store-specific credit cards. However, before you cancel them, be sure to redeem any points you have gained through the credit card's rewards program. Once you cancel the cards, the rewards are lost forever.

☐ If you need a credit card, select one card with a low spending limit so you do not overspend. Alternatively, use a reloadable pre-paid card for making purchases and ask your loved one to put a reasonable stipend on the card each month. This money should come from your personal savings or investments, not from government income.

- ☐ Give your loved one a single credit card or ATM/bank card to purchase needed items for you. This credit card should be separate from the account you have for your own personal spending.

- ☐ If you have multiple bank accounts, retirement accounts, or investments with multiple institutions, consider consolidating them as much as possible. For example, you should have one checking and savings account for personal funds, one checking and savings account for Social Security funds, one credit card for the loved one with whom you share financial control, and one institution that handles retirement accounts and investments. If you can manage to have all of these accounts through one institution, that will simplify things even more.

- ☐ If you have possessions that require insurance, such as a car or boat, and you are no longer able to use those possessions, consider selling them and canceling the insurance. This helps save money and reduces the number of bills that need to be managed. The proceeds of the sale may also substantially contribute to your personal funds.

How to Avoid Scams

Even if you take measures to protect your finances and save your funds, you may still be vulnerable to scams that prey on retirees and individuals whose health is compromised. Fraudsters target these populations because they usually have investments, a lifetime of savings, and equity in their homes. The people who perpetrate these scams are clever, and it can be difficult to recognize that they are running a scam until it is too late. To learn more about common financial scams, read the checklist below. Note that some of these scams may come in several forms.

For example, similar types of fraud may be perpetrated via mail or over the phone.

Checklist: Common types of financial scams

Mail, e-mail, and Internet scams

☐ Fake companies sell counterfeit drugs or fake "anti-aging" products online for a "special deal."

☐ Someone sends an e-mail stating that they have a fortune they are trying to get out of a corrupt country and they need your help to do it. The e-mail states that you send a small amount of money to help transfer the fortune, you will receive a large sum of money when the funds become available.

☐ A supposed government organization states that you may have claim to millions of dollars if you fill out a tax form and send in a small fee.

☐ A fake charity sends a letter asking for donations. Frequently, the fake charity uses a logo similar to a real charity so you think you are donating to a charity you trust.

☐ A fraudster sends a letter from what appears to be a legitimate company and asks you to verify your personal information.

Case No. 50212659422 FINANCIAL SERVICES & ADMINISTRATION / **STEVE WILLIAMS**

RE: AGENCY FUNDS DISTRIBUTION

ALL LISTED FUNDS ARE ASSURED PAYABLE • REPLY IMMEDIATELY

ATTENTION, STEVE WILLIAMS:

$182,569,351.00 in agency funds is available for all eligible claimants. As a United States citizen or legal resident, and provided your application is approved, you are entitled to a portion of these funds.

Moreover, upon your prompt and valid response to this Official Notification, you are assured an initial incentive payment in cash.

a) Your payment will be executed by check.
b) Your check will be sent by First Class Mail.

BE ASSURED -- THIS IS NOT A MISTAKE: If you are STEVE WILLIAMS listed herein, you are assured this initial payment in cash.

Follow the response instructions below, and your check will be sent in good order.

The Office of Financial Services and Administration (OFSA) provides these incentive funds for payment to all eligible applicants. OFSA also acts as a financial advisor to applicants seeking funds from various agencies.

CURRENTLY, THESE FUNDS TOTAL $182,569,351.00 (OVER ONE HUNDRED EIGHTY-TWO MILLION DOLLARS); AND ALL APPROVED GRANTS SHALL BE DULY AWARDED.

The deadline for issuing your incentive check shall be strictly observed. You are thus advised to respond to this Official Notification immediately and as follows:

1) Complete and detach OFSA Form 1080; 2) Enclose the fee required for grant documentation; and 3) Mail OFSA Form 1080 and your fee immediately (envelope enclosed).

Your check is assured. Do not delay your response in this matter.

SIGNED AND APPROVED THIS DAY

☐ A scammer takes bank information from a check and uses that information to make an online withdrawal from your account.

☐ You get a check in the mail that seems like free money. However, the check's fine print states that by depositing the funds, you will be enrolled in a program that charges a monthly fee. Many times, these checks bounce, so you don't get any money but are still enrolled in the program.

☐ You are sent a form to renew a subscription for a magazine you don't currently receive and still won't receive after the renewal.

☐ Someone sends a letter stating that you have won a sweepstakes or lottery, but you need to fill out a card with banking information and send it back so the money can be deposited into your account. A response to just one of these letters usually precipitates hundreds of similar letters and phone calls.

☐ A company mails crossword puzzles to you with the promise that completing the puzzles correctly and returning them with $10 or $15 will enter you in a lottery with huge prizes. The company might appeal to your vanity by complimenting your intelligence.

Phone scams

☐ A medical equipment company offers free equipment in exchange for your Medicaid number. Once the company has that number, they use it to bill Medicaid for fraudulent charges.

☐ A telemarketer calls and states that you have won a prize, sweepstakes, or lottery. The only catch is that you have to provide credit card or bank account information to collect the money. These calls usually originate from a Jamaican area code (876), even if the calls are not actually placed from Jamaica.

☐ Someone calls pretending to be a loved one in trouble and asks for money right away.

□ Someone calls pretending to be a government agency—maybe Medicaid—and asks you to verify personal information such as your bank account number, Social Security number, or Medicaid or Medicare claim numbers.

□ Someone calls pretending to be from your credit card company and says they want to ask about suspicious charges as a way of extracting your credit card number.

□ After a natural disaster, someone pretending to be from a well-known crisis charity (like the Red Cross) calls you to ask for "donations."

□ Someone calls stating that an assassination contract has been placed on you or a loved one, but if you pay a large fee, the contract will be cancelled.

□ A fake utility service calls you and says your electricity or gas is going to be turned off because of unpaid bills. The con artists may even send someone to your door to collect payment.

In-person scams

□ A salesman tells you that an amazing deal—usually an investment of some sort—is only good today, so you must make a decision immediately.

□ A repairman comes to the door, stating that he was driving by and noticed that your roof or gutters needed fixing. The fraudulent handyman might ask for payment up front and then never complete the work, or he may simply continue finding things that need to be "repaired." Disreputable local businesses sometimes attempt similar schemes.

□ You are offered a free lunch in exchange for attending a seminar. While at the seminar, you are pressured into purchasing poor or bogus investments. These investments often advertise "guaranteed" returns.

☐ A criminal tries to sell you a home security inspection in order to gain access to your residence and case it for a burglary.

Remember that not all scammers are strangers. Be wary of family members or friends whom you previously had little contact with suddenly showing up and offering to help manage your finances. In some cases, these long-lost individuals will attempt to gain access to your accounts to steal money.

Sometimes, it is easy to tell when an email, phone call, or in-person encounter is a scam. Other times it can be very difficult, at least at first. Watch for calls coming from area codes outside of the United States—particularly from Jamaica. Be suspicious of any communication that asks you to wire large sums of money to others. Keep an eye out for sudden increases in junk mail. All of these are indicators that scammers are targeting you. The following checklist offers some ideas for protecting yourself if you feel you are being targeted.

Checklist: Protecting yourself from scams

Phone scams

☐ Change your phone number to an unlisted number. Only give the number out to family, friends, and doctor's offices or other service providers that do not share or sell customers' contact information.

☐ Turn off the ringers on your phone. Set the answering machine to pick up on the first ring.

- ☐ Put anonymous call blocking on your phone so that all parties who call have to identify themselves.

- ☐ If you have caller ID, do not call back numbers from missed calls.

- ☐ Install a device on your telephone that prevents computer-generated calls (robocalls) from getting through.

- ☐ Block specific incoming phone numbers that you know are from scammers.

- ☐ Install a call blocker with "whitelist" capabilities. This device will block all calls except those from approved phone numbers already entered into the system. When setting up the blocker, only allow calls from phone numbers of trusted individuals, such as loved ones, doctor's offices, the bank, etc.

- ☐ Place your number on the Do Not Call registry either online or by calling 1-888-382-1222.

- ☐ Never give personal information over the phone.

Mail scams

- ☐ Authorize the post office to stop delivering third-class mail.

- ☐ Reduce junk mail by filling out an official form and submitting it to the following service. Make sure to include all spellings and variations of your name:

    DMAchoice
    DMA
    P.O. Box 900
    Cos Cob, CT 06807
    https://www.dmachoice.org/register.php

☐ Send an e-mail to the scammers telling them to take your name off their list, and ask them to send one reply e-mail indicating they will do this. If they won't, tell them that you will refer them to your lawyer for litigation and potential prosecution. Include your attorney's contact information in the e-mail.

In-person scams

☐ Check who is ringing your doorbell before you answer it. Find a window or other place where you can see the person but they cannot see you. If they do not have a legitimate reason for being there, like making a delivery, or if you are not expecting someone, like a service provider with whom you've scheduled an appointment, don't answer the door.

☐ Post a "no solicitors" sign on your front door. If a solicitor comes to your door, immediately report them to the police so the police can scan the neighborhood and talk to them.

☐ Call 911 if you are in immediate danger from an in-person scammer.

In spite of your best efforts, it is possible you may still be drawn in by a scammer. Don't be embarrassed—it happens to a lot of people. The individuals who perpetrate scams are clever. They understand how to prey on the emotions of their victims and, in many cases, they are adept at using technology to further their deception. The following checklist offers advice about what to do in the event that you have been scammed.

Checklist: What to do if you have been scammed

☐ Contact a local, state, or federal agency if you have been contacted by scammers.

☐ Report suspected cases of fraud to the National Consumer League's Fraud Center, or call the Federal Trade Commission's Consumer Response Center at (877) 382-4357. Mail-in complaints can be sent to:

NCL's Fraud.org
c/o National Consumers League
1701 K Street, NW, Suite 1200
Washington, DC 20006

☐ Report suspected cases of fraud to your state's attorney general.

☐ Don't give up! Scammers are persistent, so you may need to try several of these tactics multiple times, especially if the scammers have already received some money from you.

Another important step that you can take to protect yourself is to purchase identity theft protection. Identity theft protection helps monitor your Social Security number, credit card numbers, address, birth date, and other information to detect potential identity theft. The company then sends an alert to you if identity theft is detected or suspected. Some companies will even help you with the recovery processes, depending on the type of protection provided. Some policies help

Credit: Rrraum

reimburse your losses, whereas others reimburse you for money spent to complete the identity recovery. Each identity theft protection company has different sites that they monitor, different costs for services, different reports provided, and different recovery services provided, so you will need to do some research to determine which company is best for your situation. Most companies charge between $8 and $28 per month, depending on the level of services. Some companies that provide identity theft protection are in the following checklist. Note that this is not a comprehensive list. Many banks, agencies, and major insurance companies also provide identity theft protection plans.

Checklist: Companies that offer identity theft protection

- ☐ LifeLock

- ☐ LegalShield IDShield

- ☐ Identity Guard

- ☐ IdentityForce

- ☐ ID Watchdog

- ☐ IdentityIQ

- ☐ MyIDCare

- ☐ Complete ID

Checklist: Potential services provided by identity theft protection companies

- ☐ Sends alerts if identity theft is suspected

☐ Helps cancel or replace credit cards, driver's licenses, and other cards if your wallet is lost or stolen; may also provide access to emergency funds until your accounts can be restored

☐ Verifies change of address requests, especially for financial information that may have been diverted by identity thieves

☐ Removes your name from pre-approved credit card mailing lists

☐ Monitors credit card, checking, and savings accounts for cash withdrawals, balance transfers, and large purchases

☐ Notifies you if a large-scale identity breach occurs, even if it doesn't end up affecting your identity

☐ Scans for fraudulent activity associated with your Social Security number, including publishing your personal information online

☐ Monitors retirement and investment accounts for fraudulent withdrawals

☐ Monitors credit checks for fraudulent activity; credit checks are often performed if someone applies for a new credit card, bank account, cell phone account, mortgage, or other loans

☐ Monitors new application activity for bank accounts opened in your name

☐ Monitors your accounts for the addition of new account holders

☐ Monitors file sharing sites for fraudulent use of your identity

- ☐ Monitors criminal/black market websites for your data

- ☐ Scans court records for your data to prevent false convictions

- ☐ Monitors for changes to your publicly available information

- ☐ Helps restore your identity if identity theft occurs; some companies perform the restoration themselves, and some companies will guide you through the steps to restore your identity; some companies will spend up to $1 million for these activities, including legal fees, accountant fees, and investigative fees

- ☐ Provides access to three free annual credit reports

- ☐ Provides antivirus, anti-spyware, and firewall software for your computer

Identity theft protection plans do not prevent your identity from getting stolen. Instead, you will be notified more quickly that fraudulent activity has taken place so that you can remedy the situation before it gets out of control. Many people make the mistake of buying identity theft protection and then feeling like they are no longer vulnerable to scams or identity theft. Even with identity theft protection, you still need to be careful not to give out personal information to strangers. If you are a victim of identity theft, you should report the theft to the Federal Trade Commission. They will help you through the steps needed to recover from identity theft, even if you don't have identity theft protection.

Money-Saving Strategies

Whether you face long-term health challenges or not, saving money in retirement is almost as important as spending it wisely. Therefore, it is important to look for ways to save money in order to maximize your nest egg. Saving money now will make financial decisions easier in the future, especially if you are using a large share of your personal finances to fund your retirement. No matter which money-saving strategies you choose, you will thank yourself later for the money you save.

Credit: kurhan

Checklist: Strategies for saving money

☐ **Food and home care supplies.** Take advantage of sales and stock up on non-perishable items that you use frequently. Avoid purchasing items that you may not use or that may go bad before you use them. Use coupons and buy in bulk and online when it makes sense. If you use coupons, only use coupons for things you normally buy. If you use a coupon to buy something you would not normally purchase, then you are not saving money.

☐ **Clothing and household items.** Consider shopping at a Goodwill or thrift store for clothing and other needed household items. You can often find items in good condition for a cheap price by being willing to shop at secondhand stores.

☐ **Household expenses.** Review cable and telephone services to make sure you are ordering the best plans for your situation. Make sure that appropriate energy-saving strategies are being employed. Many cable and phone companies provide deals for customers who renew services, but you only get the discount if you call in and request it.

☐ **Safety.** An ounce of prevention is worth a pound of cure. Upgrade the safety of your bathroom by installing a few inexpensive items such as a toilet or shower rail and non-slip rugs. In addition, purchase other safety equipment as appropriate, such as a walker or bedrails. Many other home modifications will help you remain safe and avoid injury, thus saving money on medical bills.

☐ **Insurance coverage.** If you are not eligible for Medicare or Medicaid, check whether you can get coverage through a group plan offered by a professional organization. Alternatively, if you have a long-term illness and a loved one is acting as your primary caregiver, you might be eligible as a dependent under their health insurance policy. For non-medical insurance such as home insurance or car insurance, shop around to multiple insurance agencies to make sure you are getting the best deal.

☐ **Prescription drugs.** Look into prescription programs available in your area by visiting the National Council on Aging's BenefitsCheckUp website. Talk with your doctor about using generic prescriptions rather than brand-name drugs to save money. Many national retailers, such as Target and Walmart, as well as many regional supermarkets and pharmacies, offer certain generic drugs at vastly discounted rates. In addition, some pharmacies, such as Walgreens, offer a Prescription Savings

Club for individuals with inadequate prescription drug insurance.

☐ **AARP.** The AARP offers discounts, advocacy information, and access to community resources. Membership costs only $16 a year.

☐ **Certified Nursing Assistant (CNA) training.** If you've been diagnosed with a long-term illness, you can save a great deal of money on unskilled nursing care if a nearby loved one is willing to become a certified nursing assistant. Becoming licensed typically takes around six weeks, and your loved one can learn how to perform many personal care functions efficiently and safely.

☐ **Church communities.** Church communities frequently offer charitable and other care services for members.

Each community has different resources available, so take some time to investigate the those in your area to find ways to save money. Saving money on staples such as food and clothing as well as specialty items such as safety modifications or respite care can make a major difference in an already tight budget.

Conclusion

Managing your healthcare costs—especially if you have been diagnosed with a chronic terminal illness—can be overwhelming at times. Understanding your insurance needs and policies, your personal finances, and the resources available to you requires time to research your financial options and discuss them with trusted advisors or loved ones. No matter your health or your age, it is wise to start developing a management plan early. If you strive to understand your financial resources now, you can enjoy a stable, happy future.

About the Authors

Laura Town

Laura Town has authored numerous publications of special interest to the aging population. She has expertise in the field of finance as a co-author on Finance: Foundations of Financial Institutions and Management published by John Wiley and Sons, and she has contributed to several online nursing courses and texts. She has also written for the American Medical Writers Association, and her work has been published by the American Society of Journalists and Authors. As an editor, Laura has worked with Pearson Education, Prentice Hall, McGraw-Hill Higher Education, John Wiley and Sons, and the University of Pennsylvania to create both on-ground and online courses and texts. She is the past president of the Indiana chapter of the American Medical Writers Association (AMWA).

Karen Hoffman

Karen Hoffman received a Ph.D. in Pharmacology from the Department of Pharmacology and Experimental Neurosciences at the University of Nebraska Medical Center in Omaha, NE, where she was the recipient of an American Heart Association fellowship and several regional and national awards for her research on G protein-coupled receptor signaling in airways. She then pursued post-doctoral research projects at the University of North Carolina-Chapel Hill and the University of Kansas Medical Center, again receiving fellowships from the PhRMA Foundation and the American Heart Association, respectively. She has published research in the American Journal of Pathology, Journal of Biological Chemistry, and Journal of Pharmacology and Experimental Therapeutics. In 2012, Karen joined the editorial staff at WilliamsTown Communications, an editing firm that specializes in educational products for undergraduate- and graduate-level students. At WTC, Karen specializes in producing educational products related to the sciences and healthcare. In addition, Karen is board-certified for editing life sciences (BELS-certified).

A Note from the Authors

Thank you for purchasing our book! In 2017, 18 percent of the gross domestic product (GDP) of the United States was spent on healthcare. That number is expected to increase to 38 percent of the GDP by 2075. In addition, one in six Americans has a past-due bill for healthcare on their credit report, totaling $81 billion in debt.

Many people erroneously assume that the majority of this debt is result of terminal illness or chronic conditions in the elderly, but statistics do not support this assumption. In fact, the largest share of this debt is held by people who are 27 years old.

While that is sobering information, it highlights the fact that it is never too early to start taking charge of your healthcare spending. Understanding the options available to you—and the importance of saving money where you can—are essential no matter your age or your insurance status. We hope that the information included in this book will help you begin your journey to better financial and physical health!

If you have any questions for us, feel free to post them on Laura Town's Amazon Author Central page or reach out to via twitter: @laurawtown. We would appreciate it if you would take the time to review our book on Amazon, as our book's visibility on Amazon depends on reviews.

Additional Titles from Laura Town and Karen Hoffman

Alzheimer's Roadmap series:

Long-Term Care Insurance, Power of Attorney, Wealth Management, and Other First Steps

Dementia, Alzheimer's Disease Stages, Treatment Options, and Other Medical Considerations

Advance Directives, Durable Power of Attorney, Wills, and Other Legal Considerations

Home Safety Checklist Guide and Caregiver Resources for Medication Safety, Driving, and Wandering

Home Care, Long-term Care, Memory Care Units, and Other Living Arrangements

Caregiver Resources for Helping with Activities of Daily Living

Nutrition for Brain Health: Fighting Dementia

Caregiver Resources: From Independence to a Memory Care Unit

Resources

Insurance Resources:

Affordable Care Act Marketplace:
https://www.healthcare.gov/get-coverage/

Medicare Resources:

Centers for Medicare & Medicaid Services
7500 Security Boulevard
Baltimore, MD 21244
Phone: 877-267-2323

General information: http://medicare.gov/

Eligibility and premium calculator:
http://www.medicare.gov/eligibilitypremiumcalc/

Online application: https://secure.ssa.gov/iClaim/rib

Initial Enrollment Questionnaire:
https://www.mymedicare.gov/

Health insurance counseling from SHIP:
https://www.shiptacenter.org/

Medicare plan finder: https://www.medicare.gov/find-a-plan/questions/home.aspx

Medigap plans: https://www.medicare.gov/find-a-plan/questions/medigap-home.aspx?AspxAutoDetectCookieSupport=1

Medicare Savings Program:
http://www.medicare.gov/contacts/#resources/msps

Medicaid Resources:

General information: http://medicaid.gov/

Medicaid screener: https://www.healthcare.gov/screener/

Locate state Medicaid resources:
https://www.medicaid.gov/about-us/contact-us/contact-state-page.html

Federal poverty level:
https://www.healthcare.gov/glossary/federal-poverty-level-fpl/

PACE service areas: https://www.npaonline.org/pace-you/find-pace-program-your-neighborhood

Children's Health Insurance Program:
https://www.healthcare.gov/medicaid-chip/childrens-health-insurance-program/

Personal Finance Resources:

Thrift Savings Plans: https://www.tsp.gov/index.html

IRA minimum distribution worksheet:
http://www.irs.gov/pub/irs-tege/uniform_rmd_wksht.pdf

Social Security Resources:

Phone: 1-800-772-1213 (TTY 1-800-325-0778)

General information: https://www.ssa.gov/

Social Security retirement estimator:
http://www.ssa.gov/retire/estimator.html

Apply for Social Security benefits:
https://secure.ssa.gov/iClaim/rib

Locate local Social Security office:
https://secure.ssa.gov/ICON/main.jsp

Adult disability checklist:
http://www.ssa.gov/hlp/radr/10/ovw001-checklist.pdf

Apply for Social Security disability:
https://secure.ssa.gov/iClaim/dib

Medical release form:
http://www.socialsecurity.gov/forms/ssa-827.pdf

Supplemental Security Income screening:
http://ssabest.benefits.gov/

Military Resources:

U.S. Department of Veterans Affairs
810 Vermont Avenue, NW
Washington DC 20420
Phone: 1-800-827-1000

TRICARE: http://www.tricare.mil/

Find a local VA office:
http://www.va.gov/directory/guide/division.asp?dnum=3&isFlash=0

VA website: https://www.va.gov/

Government Resources:

SNAP eligibility:
https://www.fns.usda.gov/snap/eligibility

Administration on Aging: https://acl.gov/about-acl/administration-aging

Government benefits: http://www.benefits.gov/

National Council on Aging: http://www.ncoa.org;
http://www.benefitscheckup.org

Information Resources:

American Association of Retired Persons
Website: http://www.aarp.org

Alzheimer's Roadmap series
Purchase on Amazon:

Long-Term Care Insurance, Power of Attorney, Wealth Management, and Other First Steps

Dementia, Alzheimer's Disease Stages, Treatment Options, and Other Medical Considerations

Advance Directives, Durable Power of Attorney, Wills, and Other Legal Considerations

Home Safety Checklist Guide and Caregiver Resources for Medication Safety, Driving, and Wandering

Home Care, Long-term Care, Memory Care Units, and Other Living Arrangements

Caregiver Resources for Helping with Activities of Daily Living

Nutrition for Brain Health: Fighting Dementia

Caregiver Resources: From Independence to a Memory Care Unit

Reference List

AARP. (2018). Retrieved from http://www.aarp.org/

Acton, B. (2018). How to read a medical bill. Policygenius. Retrieved from https://www.policygenius.com/blog/how-to-read-a-hospital-bill/.

Abraham, T. (2019). No way to enforce hospital price transparency rule, CMS says. HealthCareDive.com. https://www.healthcaredive.com/news/no-way-to-enforce-hospital-price-transparency-rule-cms-says/545859/

AllLaw.com. (2019). Chapter 13 bankruptcy. Retrieved from https://www.alllaw.com/resources/bankruptcy/chapter-13

AllLaw.com. (2019). What does bankruptcy do? Retrieved from https://www.alllaw.com/articles/nolo/bankruptcy/what-does-bankruptcy-do.html

Alzheimer's Association. (2018). Retrieved from http://www.alz.org/

Alzheimers.gov. (n.d.). How to pay and plan ahead.

Alzheimer's Society. (2014). Top tips for managing money and preventing financial abuse.

American Association for Long-term Care Insurance. (2019). 2019 National long-term care insurance price index. Retrieved from http://www.aaltci.org/news/wp-content/uploads/2019/01/2019-Price-Index-LTC.pdf

American Council on Aging. (2019). How to spend down income and/or assets to become Medicaid eligible. Retrieved from https://www.medicaidplanningassistance.org/medicaid-spend-down

American Medical Association. (2015). Strategies to increase health care price transparency. Retrieved from https://www.ama-assn.org/sites/ama-assn.org/files/corp/media-browser/public/about-ama/councils/Council%20Reports/council-on-medical-service/issue-brief-strategies-increase-health-care-price-transparency.pdf

American Medical Association. (2018). Your patient wants to be a medical tourist—6 things you should do. Retrieved from https://www.ama-assn.org/delivering-care/ethics/your-patient-wants-be-medical-tourist-6-things-you-should-do

Anderson, J. (2014). Top 10 senior scams and how to avoid them. A Place for Mom. Retrieved from http://www.aplaceformom.com/blog/3-8-14-senior-scams-how-to-avoid/

Appleby, Julie. (2019). Health care price transparency rule. Kaiser Health News. Retrieved from https://khn.org/news/white-house-unveils-finalized-health-care-price-transparency-rule/

Armstrong, C. (2019). What you need to know before filing a medical bankruptcy. the balance. Retrieved from https://www.thebalance.com/what-to-know-about-filing-medical-bankruptcy-4159606

Assistant Secretary for Planning and Evaluation; U.S. Department of Health and Human Services. (n.d.). Retrieved from https://aspe.hhs.gov/

Association for Long Term Care Planning. (n.d.). Long term care insurance cost estimates. Retrieved from http://www.altcp.org/long-term-care-insurance/long-term-care-insurance-cost/.

Barron Ross. (2019). Medicare and Medicaid. Retrieved from http://www.barronross.com/long-term-care/medicare-and-medicaid/

BenefitsCheckUp. (2019). Retrieved from http://www.benefitscheckup.org

Benefits.gov. (2019). Retrieved from https://www.benefits.gov/

Block, S. (2012). Claiming an adult child as a dependent on your taxes. USA Today. Retrieved from http://usatoday30.usatoday.com/money/perfi/columnist/block/story/2012-01-30/claiming-adult-children-as-dependents-taxes/52890686/1

Bloom, E. (2019). Here's how much the average American spends on health care. CNBC.com. Retrieved from https://www.cnbc.com/2017/06/23/heres-how-much-the-average-american-spends-on-health-care.html

Bluth, R. (2016). Faced with unaffordable drug prices, tens of millions buy medicine outside U.S. Kaiser Health News. Retrieved from https://khn.org/news/faced-with-unaffordable-drug-prices-tens-of-millions-buy-medicine-outside-u-s/

Boerger, G. H. (2012). Estate planning and my house (or my parents' house) – What are the options?

Bukszpan, D. (2019). 4 common medical bill errors that can cost you. Acorns Grow. Retrieved from https://grow.acorns.com/4-common-medical-bill-errors-that-can-cost-you/

Bulkat, B. (2019). Can I eliminate medical bills in bankruptcy? AllLaw.com. Retrieved from https://www.alllaw.com/articles/nolo/bankruptcy/can-file-bankruptcy-eliminate-medical-bills.html

Bulkat, B. (2019). The Chapter 7 bankruptcy means test. AllLaw.com. Retrieved from https://www.alllaw.com/articles/nolo/bankruptcy/means-test-chapter-7-bankruptcy.html

Caplinger, D. (2018). 2019 HSA changes: Make the most of health savings accounts. Retrieved from https://www.fool.com/retirement/2018/11/17/2019-hsa-changes-make-the-most-of-health-savings-a.aspx

Caplinger, D. (2019). How much will Medicare cost you in 2019. Retrieved from https://www.fool.com/retirement/2019/01/03/how-much-will-medicare-cost-you-in-2019.aspx

Caring.com. (2019). 10 common financial scams targeting seniors. Retrieved from https://www.caring.com/caregivers/elder-abuse#10-common-financial-scams-targeting-seniors

Center for Medicare Advocacy. (n.d.). Medicare coverage for people with disabilities. Retrieved from http://www.medicareadvocacy.org/medicare-info/medicare-coverage-for-people-with-disabilities/

Center for State Rx Drug Pricing. (2018). Four more states submit bills to import prescription drugs from Canada. National Academy for State Health Policy. Retrieved from https://nashp.org/four-more-states-submit-bills-to-import-prescription-drugs-from-canada/

Centers for Disease Control and Prevention. (2016). Medical tourism. Retrieved from https://www.cdc.gov/features/medicaltourism/index.html

Centers for Disease Control and Prevention. (2017). Medical tourism. In CDC yellow book 2018. Retrieved from https://wwwnc.cdc.gov/travel/yellowbook/2018/the-pre-travel-consultation/medical-tourism

Centers for Disease Control and Prevention. (2019). Health and economic costs of chronic diseases. Retrieved from https://www.cdc.gov/chronicdisease/about/costs/index.htm

Centers for Medicare and Medicaid Services. (2018). 2019 Medicare Parts A & B Premiums and Deductibles. Retrieved from https://www.cms.gov/newsroom/fact-sheets/2019-medicare-parts-b-premiums-and-deductibles

Centers for Medicare and Medicaid Services. (2018). Dual eligible beneficiaries under the Medicare and Medicaid Programs. Retrieved from http://www.cms.gov/Outreach-and-Education/Medicare-Learning-Network-MLN/MLNProducts/downloads/Medicare_Beneficiaries_Dual_Eligibles_At_a_Glance.pdf

Chen, M. (2017). Why are Canada's prescription drugs so much cheaper than ours? The Nation. Retrieved from https://www.thenation.com/article/why-are-canadas-prescription-drugs-so-much-cheaper-than-ours/

Chernew, M., Hirth, R., and Cutler, D. (2003). Increased spending on health care: How much can the United States Afford? Retrieved from https://scholar.harvard.edu/files/cutler/files/increased_spending_on_health_care.pdf

Cleaver, J. (2017). How to choose between a revocable and irrevocable trust. Retrieved from http://money.usnews.com/money/personal-finance/mutual-funds/articles/2014/06/19/how-to-choose-between-a-revocable-and-irrevocable-trust

CNN Money. (2018). Ultimate guide to retirement. Retrieved from http://money.cnn.com/retirement/guide/annuities_basics.moneymag/

Cooper, R. (2013). Golden years can be a gold mine for scammers who target our seniors. Alzheimer's North Carolina, Inc.

Cohen, J. (2019). Trump ready to force transparency in healthcare pricing with an executive order. Forbes. https://www.forbes.com/sites/joshuacohen/2019/05/27/trump-ready-to-force-transparency-in-healthcare-pricing-with-an-executive-order/#fc7722576360

Dalen, J. E., & Alpert, J. S. Medical tourists: Incoming and outgoing. The American Journal of Medicine, 132(1), 9-10. Retrieved from https://www.amjmed.com/article/S0002-9343(18)30620-X/fulltext

Debt.org. (2019). What is Chapter 7 bankruptcy? Retrieved from https://www.debt.org/bankruptcy/chapter-7/

Defense Health Agency. (n.d.). http://www.tricare.mil/

EHealthMedicare. (n.d.) Medicare part D prescription drug plan changes for 2020. Retrieved from https://www.ehealthmedicare.com/medicare-part-d-articles/medicare-part-d-prescription-drug-plan-changes-for-2020/

ElderLawAnswers. (2016). Protecting your house from Medicaid estate recovery. Retrieved from http://www.elderlawanswers.com/protecting-your-house-from-medicaid-estate-recovery-12155

Elliott, K. R., & Moore, J. H., Jr. (2000). Cash balance pension plans: The new wave. Compensation and Working Conditions, Summer, 3-11.

Erb, K. P. (2017). What the expanded child tax credit looks like after tax reform. Retrieved from https://www.forbes.com/sites/kellyphillipserb/2017/12/21/how-will-the-expanded-child-tax-credit-look-after-tax-reform/#b10e9bb42057

FDIC. (2014). For seniors: 15 quick tips for protecting your finances. Retrieved from https://www.fdic.gov/consumers/consumer/news/cnsum13/quicktips.html

FindLaw.com. (2019). Advantages and disadvantages of Chapter 13 bankruptcy. Retrieved from https://bankruptcy.findlaw.com/chapter-13/pros-and-cons-of-declaring-bankruptcy-under-chapter-13.html

Fitch, A. (2014). How to spot 8 common medical billing errors. Nerdwallet. Retrieved from https://www.nerdwallet.com/blog/health/common-medical-billing-errors/?trk_location=ssrp&trk_query=medical%20bill%20errors&trk_page=1&trk_position=1

Frankel, M. (2018). Your 2018 guide to the health savings account. Retrieved from https://www.fool.com/retirement/2018/03/26/your-2018-guide-to-the-health-savings-account.aspx

Gibson, H. (2015). 6 keys steps of a successful medical billing process. M-Scribe® Medical Billing. Retrieved from https://www.m-scribe.com/blog/6-signs-you-have-a-great-medical-billing-process

Gelman, L. (2018). 10 wildly overinflated hospital costs you didn't know about. The Healthy. Retrieved from https://www.thehealthy.com/healthcare/health-insurance/wildly-overinflated-hospital-costs/

Glover, L. (2014). 6 questions you should ask before paying any medical bill. U.S. News and World Report. Retrieved from https://money.usnews.com/money/blogs/my-money/2014/09/08/6-questions-you-should-ask-before-paying-any-medical-bill

Glover, L. (2016). Request your medical records before you pay that hospital bill. Nerdwallet. Retrieved from https://www.nerdwallet.com/blog/health/medical-records-compare-hospital-bill/

Gooch, K. (2019). Trump pushes legislation to end 'outrageous medical bills'. Becker's Hospital Review. Retrieved from https://www.beckershospitalreview.com/finance/trump-pushes-legislation-to-end-outrageous-medical-bills.html

Hall, M. (2018). Cashing in your life insurance policy. Investopedia. Retrieved from http://www.investopedia.com/articles/pf/08/life-insurance-cash-in.asp

Healthcare.gov. (n.d.). Retrieved from https://www.healthcare.gov/

Healthcare.gov. (n.d.). Health savings account (HSA). Retrieved from https://www.healthcare.gov/glossary/health-savings-account-hsa/

Healthcare.gov. (n.d.). Why health insurance is important: Protection from high medical costs. https://www.healthcare.gov/why-coverage-is-important/protection-from-high-medical-costs/

Hellsell Fetterman. (2019). Irrevocable Trusts. Retrieved from http://www.helsell.com/faq/irrevocable-trusts/

Henry J. Kaiser Family Foundation. Medicaid income eligibility limits for adults as a percent of the federal poverty level. Retrieved from https://www.kff.org/health-reform/state-indicator/medicaid-income-eligibility-limits-for-adults-as-a-percent-of-the-federal-poverty-level/?currentTimeframe=0&sortModel=%7B%22colId%22:%22Location%22,%22sort%22:%22asc%22%7D

Hotfelder, A. (2019). Countable income for SSI. Retrieved from https://www.nolo.com/legal-encyclopedia/countable-income-ssi.html

Hughes, M. (2018). CMS's final bow: The 2019 final rule. Retrieved from https://www.webpt.com/blog/post/cms-s-final-bow-the-2019-final-rule

Hungelmann, J. (2012). Can I borrow from my life insurance policy? Bankrate. Retrieved from http://www.bankrate.com/finance/insurance/borrow-from-life-insurance-policy.aspx

Iam National Pension Fund. (n.d.). Apply for pension benefits. Retrieved from http://mypension.iamnpf.org/national-pension-plan/apply-for-pension-benefits.aspx

Identity Guard. (2015). Retrieved from http://www.identityguard.com/

Illinois Department of Healthcare and Family Services. (2019). HFS 591SP Medicaid Spenddown. Retrieved from https://www.illinois.gov/hfs/info/Brochures%20and%20Forms/Brochures/Pages/HFS591SP.aspx

Internal Revenue Service. (2019). Amount of Roth IRA contributions that you can make for 2020. Retrieved from https://www.irs.gov/retirement-plans/plan-participant-employee/amount-of-roth-ira-contributions-that-you-can-make-for-2020

Internal Revenue Service. (2019). How much can I contribute to my self-employed SEP plan if I participate in my employer's SIMPLE IRA plan? Retrieved from https://www.irs.gov/retirement-plans/how-much-can-i-contribute-to-my-self-employed-sep-plan-if-i-participate-in-my-employers-simple-ira-plan

Internal Revenue Service. (2019). Retirement topics—401(k) and profit-sharing plan contribution limits. Retrieved from https://www.irs.gov/retirement-plans/plan-participant-employee/retirement-topics-401k-and-profit-sharing-plan-contribution-limits

Internal Revenue Service. (2019). Retirement topics—SIMPLE IRA contribution limits. Retrieved from https://www.irs.gov/retirement-plans/plan-participant-employee/retirement-topics-simple-ira-contribution-limits

Internal Revenue Service. (2018). Retrieved from http://www.irs.gov/

Intuit TurboTax. (2019). Retrieved from https://turbotax.intuit.com/

Kincaid, E. The amount Americans spend on healthcare is still growing, but more and more slowly. Forbes. https://www.forbes.com/sites/elliekincaid/2018/12/06/the-amount-americans-spend-on-healthcare-is-still-growing-but-more-and-more-slowly/#7a6545c02eea

Kliff, S. (2019). A $20,243 bike crash: Zuckerberg hospital's aggressive tactics leave patients with big bills. Vox. Retrieved from https://www.vox.com/policy-and-politics/2019/1/7/18137967/er-bills-zuckerberg-san-francisco-general-hospital

Kliff, S. (2019). How to fight an outrageous medical bill, explained. Vox. Retrieved from https://www.vox.com/2019/3/22/18261698/how-to-fight-expensive-medical-bill

Kliff, S. (2018). She didn't get treated at the ER. But she got a $5,751 bill anyway. Vox. Retrieved from https://www.vox.com/2018/5/1/17261488/er-expensive-medical-bill

Konish, L. (2019). This is the real reason most Americans file for bankruptcy. CNBC.com. Retrieved from https://www.cnbc.com/2019/02/11/this-is-the-real-reason-most-americans-file-for-bankruptcy.html

Konrad, W. (2019). Surprise medical bills sending consumers into shock—here's how to avoid getting hit. CBS News. Retrieved from https://www.cbsnews.com/news/surprise-medical-bills-send-you-into-shock-how-to-avoid-getting-hit/

Landen, R. (2014). Pattern of problems with the Veterans Affairs healthcare system. Modern Healthcare. Retrieved from http://www.modernhealthcare.com/article/20140507/NEWS/305079939

LifeLock. (2019). Retrieved from https://www.lifelock.com/

Loth, R. (n.d.). Retirement plans. Investopedia. Retrieved from http://www.investopedia.com/university/retirementplans/

Madara, J. L. (2018). Price transparency. American Medical Association. Retrieved from https://searchlf.ama-assn.org/undefined/documentDownload?uri=%2Funstructured%2Fbinary%2Fletter%2FLETTERS%2F2018-3-23-Price-Transparency.pdf

MB-Guide.org. (2019). The medical billing process – step by step. Retrieved from http://www.mb-guide.org/medical-billing-process2.html

McCoy, M. (2019). 8 ways to save on the cost of prescription drugs. Money Crashers. Retrieved from https://www.moneycrashers.com/ways-save-cost-prescription-drugs/

Medicaid.gov. (2019). Retrieved from http://www.medicaid.gov/

Medical Bill Rehab LLC. (2019). 7 common medical billing errors. Retrieved from https://www.medicalbillrehab.com/7-common-medical-billing-errors/.

MedicalBillingAndCoding.org. (2018). Everything you need to get started in medical billing & coding. Retrieved from https://www.medicalbillingandcoding.org/billing-process/.

Medical Tourism Association. (2019). Medical tourism FAQ's. Retrieved from https://www.medicaltourismassociation.com/en/medical-tourism-faq-s.html

Medicaid.gov. (2019). SSI and spousal impoverishment standards. Retrieved from https://www.medicaid.gov/medicaid/eligibility/downloads/spousal-impoverishment/ssi-and-spousal-impoverishment-standards.pdf

Medicare.gov. (2019). Find your level of extra help (part D). Retrieved from https://www.medicare.gov/your-medicare-costs/get-help-paying-costs/find-your-level-of-extra-help-part-d

Medicare.gov. (2019). Medicare costs at a glance. Retrieved from https://www.medicare.gov/your-medicare-costs/medicare-costs-at-a-glance

Medicare.gov. (n.d.) Physical therapy. Retrieved from https://www.medicare.gov/coverage/physical-therapy

Medicare.gov. (n.d.) Procedure price lookup. Retrieved from https://www.medicare.gov/procedure-price-lookup/

Medicare.gov. (2019). Retrieved from http://www.medicare.gov/

MedicareInteractive.org. (2019). Returning to a SNF after leaving. Retrieved from https://www.medicareinteractive.org/get-answers/medicare-covered-services/skilled-nursing-facility-snf-services/returning-to-a-snf-after-leaving

MedicareInteractive.org. (2019). Spend-down program for beneficiaries with incomes over the Medicaid limit. Retrieved from https://www.medicareinteractive.org/get-answers/cost-saving-programs-for-people-with-medicare/medicare-and-medicaid/spend-down-program-for-beneficiaries-with-incomes-over-the-medicaid-limit

Medicare Today. (2018). Fact sheet: Medicare Part D Extra Help program in 2019. Retrieved from http://medicaretoday.org/wp-content/uploads/2018/09/Medicare-Part-D-Extra-Help-Program-in-2019.pdf

Michon, K. (2019). Paying your bankruptcy lawyer: Costs & types of fees. AllLaw.com. Retrieved from https://www.alllaw.com/articles/nolo/bankruptcy/paying-lawyer-attorney-fees.html

Michon, K. (2019). Steps in a Chapter 13 bankruptcy case. AllLaw.com. Retrieved from https://www.alllaw.com/articles/nolo/bankruptcy/steps-chapter-13.html

Military.com. (2019). Retrieved from http://www.military.com/benefits/tricare

Mooney, S. M. (n.d.). Life estate ownership of real estate. Retrieved from http://www.susanmooney.com/?page_id=530

National Association of Counties. (2019). Governance. Retrieved from https://www.naco.org/governance

National Center for Employee Ownership. (2018). ESOP Facts. Retrieved from http://www.esop.org/

National Council on Aging. (n.d.) How much does Medicare Part D cost? Retrieved from https://www.mymedicarematters.org/costs/part-d/

National Heart, Lung, and Blood Institute. (2013). Reduce screen time. Retrieved from https://www.nhlbi.nih.gov/health/educational/wecan/reduce-screen-time/

National Institute on Aging. (2017). Managing money problems in Alzheimer's disease. Retrieved from https://www.nia.nih.gov/health/managing-money-problems-alzheimers-disease

National Reverse Mortgage Lenders Association. (2019). Your guide to reverse mortgages. Retrieved from http://www.reversemortgage.org/

New York State Department of Health. (2010). Medicaid Excess Income ("spenddown" or "surplus income") program. Retrieved from https://www.health.ny.gov/health_care/medicaid/excess_income.htm

NOLO. (n.d.). Are revocable or irrevocable living trusts useful in qualifying for Medicaid? Retrieved from http://www.nolo.com/legal-encyclopedia/are-revocable-irrevocable-living-trusts-useful-qualifying-medicaid.html

NOLO. (2019). How does Medicaid's Medically Needy program work? Retrieved from https://www.nolo.com/legal-encyclopedia/how-does-medicaids-medically-needy-program-work.html

NOLO. (2019). Income and asset limits for SSI Disability eligibility. Retrieved from https://www.nolo.com/legal-encyclopedia/income-asset-limits-ssi-disability-eligibility.html

Office of the Assistant Secretary for Planning and Evaluation. (n.d.). 2019 poverty guidelines. Retrieved from https://aspe.hhs.gov/2019-poverty-guidelines

Pabian & Russell, LLC. (n.d.). Irrevocable asset protection trust. Retrieved from http://www.pabianrussell.com/Elder-Law/irrevocable-asset-protection-trust

Paying for Senior Care. (2016). Alzheimer's costs by state. Retrieved from https://www.payingforseniorcare.com/alzheimers/financial-assistance.html#title15

Q1Medicare.com. (n.d.) 2019 Medicare Part D outlook. Retrieved from https://q1medicare.com/PartD-The-2019-Medicare-Part-D-Outlook.php

Q1Medicare.com. (n.d.) Understanding the 2019 medicare part D

coverage gap or donut hole. Retrieved from
https://q1medicare.com/q1group/MedicareAdvantagePartD/Blog.php
?blog=Understanding-the-2019-Medicare-Part-D-Coverage-Gap-or-
Donut-Hole&blog_id=712&category_id=9

Radcliffe, S. (2019). Concerned about getting Rx drugs from Canada?
Here's what to know. Healthline. Retrieved from
https://www.healthline.com/health-news/fda-sends-warning-to-
canadian-drug-company-what-to-know

RevCycleIntelligence.com. (2019). Going Above and Beyond the CMS
Hospital Price Transparency Rule. Retrieved from
https://revcycleintelligence.com/features/going-above-and-beyond-
the-cms-hospital-price-transparency-rule

Riggs, M. (2018). Are Canadian pharmacies the solution to America's
high prescription drug prices? Reason. Retrieved from
https://reason.com/2018/01/03/are-canadian-pharmacies-the-
solution-to/

RothIRA.com. (n.d.). 2018 Roth IRA rules – eligibility, income,
contribution limits, and more.

San Medical Billing. (2017). 10 steps of medical billing process. Medium.
Retrieved from https://medium.com/@sanmedicalbilli/10-steps-of-
medical-billing-process-e6548ba5b17a

Santhanam, L. (2018). Millennials rack up the most medical debt, and
more frequently. PBS News Hour. Retrieved from
https://www.pbs.org/newshour/health/millennials-rack-up-the-most-
medical-debt-and-more-frequently

SeniorLiving.org. (2019). Nursing home costs. Retrieved from
https://www.seniorliving.org/nursing-homes/costs/

Sherman, F. (2018). Should I put my house into an irrevocable trust?
Retrieved from http://homeguides.sfgate.com/should-put-house-
irrevocable-trust-72197.html

Social Security Administration. (2019). Retrieved from
http://www.ssa.gov/

Social Security Administration. (n.d.). Benefits planner: Retirement. Retrieved from https://www.ssa.gov/planners/retire/agereduction.html

Social Security Administration. (n.d.). Extra help with medicare prescription drug plan costs: What help can I received? Retrieved from https://www.ssa.gov/benefits/medicare/prescriptionhelp/

Social Security Administration. (2019). Research, statistics & policy analysis. Retrieved from https://www.ssa.gov/policy/docs/quickfacts/prog_highlights/RatesLimits2020.html

Social Security Administration. (n.d.). SSI federal payment amounts for 2020. Retrieved from https://www.ssa.gov/oact/cola/SSI.html

South Dakota Office of the Attorney General. (n.d.). Durable power of attorney. Retrieved from https://atg.sd.gov/victim/seniors/powerofattorney.aspx

Steele, J. (2018). Maximizing points and miles on healthcare spending. The Points Guy. Retrieved from https://thepointsguy.com/guide/maximizing-points-and-miles-on-healthcare-spending/

Steussy, L. (2019). Man shows shocking health care cost of his attempted suicide. New York Post. Retrieved from https://nypost.com/2019/04/18/this-is-how-expensive-it-is-to-attempt-suicide-in-the-us-viral-post/

TheBankruptcySite.org. (2019). How medical bills are treated in Chapter 13 bankruptcy. Retrieved from https://www.thebankruptcysite.org/resources/bankruptcy/filing-bankruptcy/can-i-file-bankruptcy-medical-bills

The Finance Buff. (2018). 2018 2019 401k 403b IRA contribution limits. Retrieved from https://thefinancebuff.com/401k-403b-ira-contribution-limits.html

Thrift Savings Plan. (2019). Contribution limits. Retrieved from https://www.tsp.gov/PlanParticipation/EligibilityAndContributions/contributionLimits.html

Transportation Security Administration. (2014). TSA travel tips—traveling with medication. Retrieved from https://www.tsa.gov/blog/2014/09/05/tsa-travel-tips-traveling-medication

United States Department of Agriculture, Food and Nutrition Service. (2018). Supplemental Nutrition Assistance Program (SNAP). Retrieved from https://www.fns.usda.gov/snap/snap-special-rules-elderly-or-disabled

United States Department of Defense. (n.d.). Military Compensation. Retrieved from http://militarypay.defense.gov/retirement/

United States Department of Labor. (n.d.). http://www.dol.gov/

United States Department of Veterans Affairs. (n.d.). Retrieved from http://www.va.gov/

U.S. Customs and Border Protection. (2019). Prohibited and restricted items. Retrieved from https://www.cbp.gov/travel/us-citizens/know-before-you-go/prohibited-and-restricted-items

U.S. Department of State—Bureau of Consular Affairs. (2018). Traveler's checklist. Retrieved from https://travel.state.gov/content/travel/en/international-travel/before-you-go/travelers-checklist.html

U.S. Department of Health and Human Services. (2019). Physical activity guidelines for Americans. Retrieved from https://www.hhs.gov/fitness/be-active/physical-activity-guidelines-for-americans/index.html

U.S. Food & Drug Administration. (2016). 5 tips for traveling to the U.S. with Medications. Retrieved from https://www.fda.gov/consumers/consumer-updates/5-tips-traveling-us-medications

Verma, S. (n.d.). You have the right to know the price. Centers for Medicare and Medicaid Services. Retrieved from https://www.cms.gov/blog/you-have-right-know-price

Wells Fargo Advisors. (2019). Wealth transfer. Retrieved from https://www.wellsfargoadvisors.com/planning/goals/wealth-transfer.htm?linknav=topnav:planLife:helpPlan:wealthTransfer

Whole30.com. (2019). The Whole30® program. Retrieved from https://whole30.com/whole30-program-rules/

Woodruff, M. (2013). Costco's prescription drug prices can't be beat. Business Insider. Retrieved from https://www.businessinsider.com/prescription-drugs-cheaper-at-costco-vs-cvs-2013-4

Eat Right, Fight Dementia

NUTRITION FOR BRAIN HEALTH
Fighting Dementia

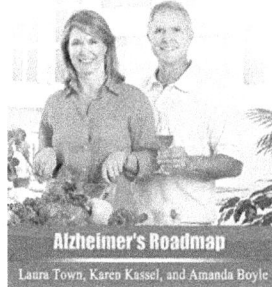

Alzheimer's Roadmap

Laura Town, Karen Kassel, and Amanda Boyle

Nutrition for Brain Health: Fighting Dementia provides answers to the following questions and more:

- **How can what I eat affect my brain health?** Discover how to lower your risk factors for dementia by decreasing your intake of saturated fats and cholesterol, balancing your diet, and controlling the calories you consume.
- **Do I need to exercise?** Explore the various ways that everyday activities can double as brain-enhancing exercise and improve your total health as well.
- **Does what I drink matter?** Find out how some things you may drink, such as coffee, tea, or red wine, can actually be beneficial for brain health in moderation.
- **How do I get the vitamins I need?** Know what dietary and lifestyle choices can increase your intake of essential vitamins such as vitamins C and B_{12}.
- **Is there an electronic version of this book?** Yes, and it's free! You can find it at: https://adbl.co/2Vwbe0d

www.ingramcontent.com/pod-product-compliance
Lightning Source LLC
Chambersburg PA
CBHW022036190326
41520CB00008B/599